AN AFRICAN JOURNEY

▼

AN AFRICAN JOURNEY

Stories and Photographs

BY MARK PATINKIN

▼

WILLIAM B. EERDMANS PUBLISHING COMPANY
GRAND RAPIDS, MICHIGAN

Front cover: A child in a feeding camp in Mali.
Back cover: Crossing an arm of the Niger River near Timbuktu.

© 1985 The Providence Journal Company

This material originally appeared in the
Providence Journal-Bulletin

This edition published 1985 through special
arrangement with the Providence Journal Company
by William B. Eerdmans Publishing Company
255 Jefferson Ave. S.E., Grand Rapids, Mich. 49503

Art Director, RAY LOMAX
Photo Editor, MICK COCHRAN
Designer, CHRISTIAN POTTER DRURY

Library of Congress Cataloging-in-Publication Data

Patinkin, Mark.
   An African journey.

   1. Africa, Sub-Saharan — Description and travel —
1981-   . 2. Sahel — Description and travel.
3. Droughts — Sahel. 4. Patinkin, Mark. I. Title.
DT352.2.P37   1985   916   85-15987

ISBN 0-8028-0162-5

Foreword

The man who runs my paper's newsroom is named Chuck Hauser. We were having lunch when he asked if there was anything new I'd like to try with the column I write. Like any reporter, the first thing that came to mind was travel. He asked where.

"I don't know," I said. "I've been reading about Ethiopia lately. But I know that's pretty far."

I then suggested some more realistic trips. Maybe an occasional story in New York. Washington. I didn't mention Ethiopia again, and even dropped it from my own mind. Newspapers don't send columnists on foreign assignments.

That was on a Friday. On Monday, shortly after I walked into the newsroom, another editor called me over.

"Chuck wants you to go to Africa," he said.

It's what the best of editors are about - they're able to see which door a writer should walk through, even before the writer sees it. This project was Chuck Hauser's idea even more than mine, and a piece of it belongs to him.

It belongs to a few other people, too.

Getting these stories into the Providence Journal, where they first appeared, was almost as hard as getting the stories. Usually, when on the road, we dictate by phone. You can't do that in a continent where most phones don't work. The only choice was to telex them. Telexes are machines usually used by businessmen to send 30-second notes overseas. They limit them to 30 seconds because it's not cheap. My stories took about 40 minutes each.

The machines were bears to work. Most were in hotel offices and looked like old supermarket cash registers. After I'd compose my columns on a portable computer I'd brought along, it often took three hours more to retype each onto the telex before pushing the send button. They'd arrive in a computer bank in the midwest. There was no way the Journal could tell when a story got there, so throughout my trip, Linda Rasmanis and Gordon Smith, who work in our systems division, would spend their days checking the computer bank every hour or so. When they fetched out a dispatch, they'd send it over to my key editor, Joel Rawson.

If anyone gave a pint or two of blood to this project, it was him. The telexes put every letter of my stories in capitals. They often sent without paragraphs. On the French side of Africa, the keyboards even had a few letters in the wrong place. I sometimes ended up typing each A as a Q, each M as a W. Worse, the transmission often garbled entire sections. Linda would have to cable back to my hotel, sometimes on deadline, asking what I was trying to say. I'd have to resend paragraphs for Rawson to plug in. It took him up to five hours to refine each piece, and there was no way he could put it off until tomorrow - we were writing daily. There were other editors who often gave their time to putting my stories into shape. Mark Silverman, our Sunday editor, was one. Len Levin, Mike Young and Andy Burkhardt, daily editors, were three others.

For Rawson, it was more than clerical labor. He also cut out an occasional sentence or paragraph, sometimes refining ragged prose. Writers usually hate seeing their stuff tampered with that way. Being 7,000 miles away, I was unable to protest. When I got back home and finally saw his refinements, I had a reaction reporters almost never do.

"Gee," I thought, "that reads better."

I happen to have a writer's ego. It makes it hard for me to understand how those behind the scenes, who get no glory, can invest so much of themselves into making us look good. It brings me to the three people instrumental in putting together this book.

Ray Lomax, the Journal's art director, first saw the photos on a Friday. He later told me he was so drawn to the project he couldn't sleep that night, and came in Saturday, on his own time, to begin the design. I spent hours with Mick Cochran, our Sunday photo editor, sifting through 400 pictures. He, too, got caught up, arguing for selections as if they were his own. Then there was Christian Drury, who did both of those jobs, giving her nights and weekends to shepherd this book with a concern for detail even beyond my own.

Many of the nation's big newspapers sent reporters to Africa, but usually for only one or two weeks, and in most cases, to only one country. I was one of few who spent a month crossing the whole continent, writing in journey form. It was not a cheap undertaking. Neither was this book. The resources for all of it were provided by the Providence Journal's publisher, Michael Metcalf.

"An African Journey" was at first distributed only in Rhode Island. It seemed for a while it would go no further. I approached almost 50 publishers about taking it national, and while many came close, they decided it would have to be put out quickly, between their quarterly lists, and that would be too disruptive. Then I got a call from Bill Eerdmans, president of Eerdmans Publishing Company. Yes, he said, taking on this book would be disruptive, but he and Jon Pott, his editor-in-chief, felt the cause was one worth pushing for.

I happened to be the point man for this journey. But the vision behind it belongs to all of us.

■■■ **M.P.**

▲

Prologue
Thursday, November 29, 1984

I have been planning this trip for three weeks now. I will be gone for a month, to Africa, to write about the famine. My plane leaves for Ethiopia tomorrow. At the moment, I am not sure I will be on it.

There is one arrangement still unresolved. Not the travel itinerary; I've confirmed a string of flights into five countries. I've confirmed hotels, too. I've even set up interviews with relief workers at refugee camps. I am missing only one thing. Permission to get into the continent. I have yet to be given a visa to Ethiopia.

"No," he said. "Please don't come without a visa. Journalists who do this are sent back."

It is almost 1 in the morning as I write this. I sit by my phone, waiting for 9 a.m. in Addis Ababa. That is when Ethiopia's government ministries open. I have been up this late all week, calling across an ocean, hoping I'll get just the right bureaucrat, one who speaks English, someone with the power to tell their Washington embassy that yes, this journalist can be let in.

I place a call. A recording tells me all lines into the country are busy. I try again every few minutes for almost an hour. Finally, I get through. A voice answers. He promises to help, but cautions that three ministries have to approve before their embassy can stamp my passport.

"My plane leaves in 36 hours," I tell him.

"No," he says. "Please don't come without a visa. Journalists who do this are sent back."

When the paper decided to have me write about drought in Africa, I thought there would be an open door into any country I chose. Famine is one area where the media do make a difference. The more publicity, the more donations. I figured I'd be able to leave for Ethiopia in days.

To make sure, I flew to Washington to apply for a visa in person. The aide in the embassy thanked me, then said he didn't have the power to give me permission. No one there did. I'd have to get Ethiopia to cable authorization myself. I asked whom I should cable. The Foreign Ministry, he said, and thanked me for my interest.

How do you work the Addis Ababa bureaucracy from Providence, Rhode Island? I began with Senator Pell's office. I was referred to the African specialist on his Foreign Relations staff, a Rhode Island native named Nancy Stetson. I figured I was home. I now had the power of the U.S. Senate behind me. Stetson told me she would do her best, and did end up giving me hours of her time, but there was a problem. Ethiopia is a Soviet ally that has not had formal ties with America in years. Although relations are warming because of U.S. food aid, Marxist governments are cautious about journalists.

I spent up to six hours a day on the phone, all on the visa chase, finally catching a Christian Science Monitor correspondent in the Associated Press office in nearby Nairobi, Kenya. He'd just been to Ethiopia, and told me he had to wait a month for a visa. But he gave me the name of a government official who might help: Mr. Teklu, of the Ministry of Information. I began sending him regular telexes. Finally, one night at 2 a.m. my time, I got him by phone. He was gracious, but told me it would take time.

Meanwhile, as it became clear the famine runs throughout Africa, I decided to try visiting four other countries. That meant four other visas. Four more Washington embassies to apply to. If I used the mail, it could take months. Then I found there are such things as visa services. They do it for you. The man I got, David Hickman, had never handled a journalist before.

"No problem," he said when he first took me on.

It turns out journalists are more difficult than he thought. African countries don't like journalists.

"I can't wait until this job is over," Hickman told me after two weeks.

I got a similar reaction from my travel agent. I felt I had no choice but to begin booking flights, visa or no visa. The agent mapped out a plan for me. It was full of midnight departures, standard for Africa. I zeroed in on one hectic day and asked what would happen if I missed the plane. I hoped I wouldn't have to wait too many hours for another one.

"The next plane is a week later," she said.

Getting between African cities on a sane schedule turned out to be so tricky I had to cancel certain countries and choose new ones. That meant getting my visa service to send me new applications by Federal Express. It meant telling my travel agent three times to tear up the itinerary she'd arranged and start over.

"Have a wonderful weekend," she said sweetly one Friday. "And don't call me again until Monday."

I'd allowed myself three weeks to get the visas. Slowly, one by one, they came through. All but Ethiopia.

That's when I began the 1 a.m. calls. I got Mr. Teklu again as Sunday turned into early Monday. He said it looked as though it would happen in 24 hours. That would mean I'd get it only two days before my plane. Twenty-four hours passed, no visa. Forty-eight, still nothing. If I missed the plane, the whole thing would have to be pushed back weeks. I briefly considered flying in without a visa, presuming I could talk my way by. Then I read of a Philadelphia Inquirer reporter who tried that. They sent him back to Philadelphia.

Tuesday at midnight, I began working the phones again. By 2 a.m., I'd reached three ministries, and did everything but beg. Actually, maybe I did beg. They said they'd do their best. Six hours later, I dialed the Washington embassy. The woman I'd been badgering daily answered.

"Any luck?" I asked.

"Finally," she said.

My visa service got the stamp. Federal Express is due to have the passport in Providence at 10:30 today. My plane leaves for JFK about two hours later.

I am told it will be difficult over there. I am told reporters spend 80 percent of their time getting government papers and only 20 percent seeing what they've come to see. I'm told most Westerners end up physically sick because of food and conditions. The phones are bad, often making it impossible to send back stories. The roads are bad, too - it can take 12 or even 24 hours to travel 100 miles by jeep. I could have drawn better assignments. But few as worthwhile. Some things, we should know about. ▮

" I asked what would happen if I missed the plane. I hoped I wouldn't have to wait too many hours for another one.'The next plane is a week later,' she said."

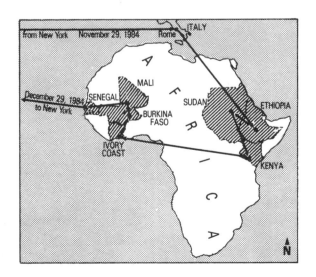

▲

Sunday, December 9, 1984

ADDIS ABABA, Ethiopia - It is a strange mission I've come on. I've come in search of starvation. I've never seen anything close to it before. Most Americans haven't. Maybe poverty, or violence, but not famine, not of this scope. Starvation is something we don't know about.

I have come a bit late. They say more than 300,000 have died here in the last year. Now, suddenly, this past month, it has become news. It is as if World War II had been discovered in 1943.

I have never been near a war, but it strikes me that living behind the lines must be something like this. Constantly, there are reports from the front. Death tolls.

We journalists are all following maps. I now know the names of Ethiopia's drought towns, and how long it takes to reach them, almost as well as my own state.

Axum, yes, that's getting better. And Alamata. But Mekele is getting bad again. And Bati, the new camp, it is very bad now. A month ago it did not exist. Now, there are 25,000 there.

" There are two sides to this country. There are the soldiers, the bureaucracy, the pictures of Lenin. And there are the people. It was becoming clear to me which is Ethiopia's soul."

Then, of course, there is Korem. The true horror. Almost 60,000 in Korem. Many of them enduring 40-degree nights without shelter. Or even blankets. Thirty and more dying a day. Two days of food left, no more in the port, and from the countryside, the hungry continue to come in.

I arrive in Addis at 8 a.m., overnight from Rome. It is truly an African city, a wedding of East and West. Mercedes and donkeys move together through downtown streets. At every stop, a child appears at my taxi window. The words are always the same.

"Very hungry," they say. "Very poor. No eat in two days."

When I tell them I have no local coins, guiltily showing travelers checks, they thank me and bow.

It usually takes eight days for a journalist to get travel papers in Ethiopia, but I cannot afford that. I am here for only a week. I go straight to the Ministry of Information. The officials there recognize my name. Yes, you're the reporter who called so often from America. We'll try to do it fast. Maybe tomorrow, they say.

I head to the Addis Hilton, where I am told my reservation has fallen through. I find another hotel where the phone does not work and then spend the afternoon waiting in various ministries.

The next day, with the sun, I begin my rounds a second time.

Maybe tomorrow, they say.

I am finding out that this is one of Africa's most often used phrases.

I turn my attention to transport. Other reporters tell me it is even harder than papers. There are few flights and, understandably, the priority is supplies, not journalists. Flying time is 90 minutes north, where there are no airports, just dirt strips which are themselves an hour by car from the camps. Over bad roads.

On my third day, a breakthrough. I call the British Royal Air Force at dawn. They've been running mercy flights daily and now tell me they may have room at 10 a.m. At 8, I am back at the Ministry of Information. By now I know the assistant director well. I tell him this is my only chance. He smiles at my desperation. Because you called so often from America, he says, we will try. Incredibly, he agrees to send an aide to the Ministry of Security to plead my case.

I go with him, as does a woman relief worker who has herself been waiting a week in Addis. We arrive outside the gate. The aide looks nervous - this is a forbidden place, surrounded by barbed wire. He tells us to come back in two hours. We tell him we'd rather wait right here. Eight a.m. turns into 9, then 9:30. The security guards, holding machine guns, stare at me in silence.

Ten o'clock, comes and goes - RAF takeoff time. At 10:15, too late, my papers arrive.

I suppose it sounds cold to talk about travel problems in the midst of such tragedy, but even the relief workers speak of little else. They, too, spend as much time getting to their jobs as doing them. One does not move easily in a socialist country. Deep down, we hope our work will help, but on the surface, the reality of the Westerner in the Third World is to be obsessed, and often defeated, by logistics.

Soon I get back into the Hilton. The sign on top of it reads "Peace, Friendship, Solidarity." Nearby, there is a huge statue of Lenin.

But it's still a Hilton. Throughout the day and evening, I can hear the sound of tennis balls being hit outside. The pool is crowded. There are generous buffets. At night, the staff turns down your sheets and leaves a piece of chocolate on the pillow.

I guess it's a cliche to talk about the hotel of luxury in the land of poverty, but right now, it's hard to believe I'm here to cover a famine of Biblical proportion.

Still, if you listen closely, even in Addis, you can hear echoes of what is happening.

On the streets, men pull you into corners to offer antique jewelry - of silver - for $5. It is common knowledge most of it has filtered down from the north, where the desperate have sold everything to survive.

On my way out one day, I recognize a woman unloading gear from a taxi. Her name is Claire Bertsienger, the Swiss Red Cross worker who'd been the centerpiece of the 60 Minutes report on Ethiopia. She tells me she's just arrived from five weeks in one of the camps. She planned to spend the afternoon in a bath. Actually, she looked very fresh. It was not a physical cleansing she was after.

The next day, I wake up feeling I've spent too many days in hotels and bureaucracies. It is too much.

I head outside to find Ethiopia, walking alone toward the netherside of the city, where the houses are not houses, or even shacks, just huts of thatch and mud.

I am not sure how I will be recieved: a healthy American walking amidst poverty in a Soviet protectorate. On every block, there are thousands of people, living like I've never seen people live. It occurs to me that the clothes I wear, although basic, are still worth more than the $120 the average Ethiopian earns in a year. They have reason for hatred, or at least resentment.

All I got were smiles. And waves.

Soon, children began to gather. Five, a dozen, maybe 30. I was carrying my passport and all my money, I was the only white face in this most difficult of black ghettos, and I did not feel at all threatened. I had not expected that of Ethiopia.

Two of the children stayed with me as I moved from block to block.

"I show you," said one. "I show you Gabriel Church. No problem."

It was a half-mile walk. They held onto my hands the whole time. When we got there, the one called David pointed to the building, proud of its beauty. I paused to stare at

The two street kids who showed me Addis.

something the two children did not notice, perhaps because they were used to it.

The grounds were full of blind people. Old women, mostly. Their ears served them. They heard my English and moved toward me, holding out their hands. I took out some coins and handed them to the closest one. The others heard, and grabbed, and began to fight. Quickly, the two boys led me away.

The three of us spent two hours together that afternoon. They carried my camera. They showed me Addis. They fell silent only when we passed soldiers, which was often. The soldiers all carried Soviet rifles.

The boys took me to a second church. Outside, a young man approached, asking if

From the Addis Hilton, I could see the city's contrast - clay tennis courts alongside thatch hut slums.

I'd like a tour. He was businesslike and wary until we got away from the door and the crowds, inside, to a secluded corner beneath a stained glass window. Then he turned to me. You are from where, he asked. America, I said. What he did next both embarrassed and touched me.

He bent deep and for long seconds, he held my hand against his forehead.

"America," he said. "America."

There are two sides to this country. There are the soldiers, the bureaucracy, the pictures of Lenin. And there are the people. It was becoming clear to me which is Ethiopia's soul.

As the children and I walked back to the Hilton, a man in a suit approached. He noticed my cameras. "You are American journalist," he said.

I nodded.

"If you had not been here, God knows what would have happened with the hungry people. Please tell the world. You are welcome. Welcome."

It surprised me. No Ethiopian I'd met in passing had yet mentioned the famine to me. The government restricts information on it. I was beginning to think many did not know. But they do know. It is just that they must be careful here.

The man continued to thank me for coming here. Then he looked past my shoulder. Two soldiers had walked into view.

"I take a risk talking this way," he said. "I must go. You are welcome."

Two Ethiopias.

There is one more thing you should know. When the children and I entered the grounds of one of the churches, some elderly men approached from the gate. The children told me it was tradition to give each a coin. All I had were Ethiopian bills worth $5. I began to take one from my wallet.

"No, no," whispered one of the boys. "Too much."

I told him it was all I had, and that it was all right.

"Too much," he said. "No problem."

As far as I could tell, the child was destitute. And still, he took coins from his pocket and placed them in the palms of the five men. Afterward, I tried to press a $5 bill into his hand. He would not take it. "No problem," he said. "No problem."

There has been some debate about our obligation to aid a Russian ally that hamstrings Westerners who come to help. I had wondered about it myself.

Now, I understood what this mission, and our role, is about. It is about the people, not the government. And mostly, it is about the children. ■

Monday, December 10, 1984 ▼

ADDIS ABABA, Ethiopia - My third day in Ethiopia has passed. I spent it, like the first two, trying to move from the capital, and failing. If I've felt this kind of frustration before, I can't remember it. The time, though, has not been a waste. Three weeks from now, when I am heading home, I think I will still look back on my first hours overseas as one of the important parts of this trip.

I met her in Rome. She is one of three Americans in Italy with ambassador rank. It is why I presumed she would not have time for me. The embassy said not to count on it, it was a bad day for her.

As it turned out, she gave me more than two hours.

I'd forgotten that Millicent Fenwick smokes a pipe. As soon as we sat down, she began digging into her purse. I expected her to pull out notes, or glasses, or whatever women in their 70s keep in purses. Instead, she took out a pouch of tobacco.

"You still have the pipe," I said.

"Oh," she said, "I haven't changed, you know."

I still think of her as Lacey Davenport. That is the Doonesbury character based on Millicent Fenwick. Both were kind, elderly congresswomen with an unlikely mix - superior breeding and an outrage at injustice.

Like many Americans, I had a vague memory of her taking some obscure post overseas. I had no idea what it involved, until I began researching this trip and found it involved feeding the hungry.

She is ambassador to the United Nations Food and Agriculture Organization, something I've also never heard of. It turns out to be a major force in the world we rarely think about, the Third World. It's housed in a complex in Rome the size of the U.N. Its mission is to solve what many non-Americans feel is the issue of our time - boosting food production where there is too little of it. It is why I wanted to meet Ambassador Fenwick - her focus, this month, is my focus.

There was a more personal reason, too. I wanted to know why a woman who'd once been near the spotlight's center would embrace an issue so low on our national agenda, so far from home.

The day I got there, the FAO was in its annual summit. The morning session broke at 12:30. Fenwick was the last to leave, lingering for 40 minutes to argue a point with four other delegates. I noticed she was a toucher. She kept grabbing her colleagues' arms, jabbing her glasses at them. Or her pipe. I know few Americans who can get that worked up over farming in Tanzania.

She had a surprisingly firm handshake. She asked me how many days I'd be in Rome. I told her I was on the midnight flight to Addis. In that case, she said, we'd have to go to one of her favorite restaurants.

We took a table near the windows. I asked her how often she gets to the states. I presumed ambassadors jet overseas regularly.

"Once a year," she said.

"That's all?"

"I don't want to lean on the taxpayers more than is right."

As soon as we'd ordered, I asked the question that most interested me.

How did she move from Congress to the Third World? It happened after her 1982 defeat. The White House asked if she would

---

" She came up with a quote from a rabbi she had known. 'You will never arrive at the solution,' he told her. 'You will never be absolved of the responsibility of trying.' "

7

serve in some way. She said she wasn't sure. She'd decided it might be time to have her life back. They mentioned a few posts anyway. They didn't interest her.

Then the FAO came up. Would she be ambassador? She knew only what the surface of it involved. She did not like the idea of being alone overseas.

And she took it right away.

I asked why. She went back 45 years to explain what first drew her to public affairs. "Hitler did," she said. "It was unbearable seeing such injustice." In a very different way, this issue touched the same part of her.

Some things, she said, cannot be tolerated. She seems to have only one hatred in her, for unfairness.

"But this isn't neccessarily America's responsibility," I said.

She took me by the arm. "A decent society doesn't stand by and watch people die when there are enormous stores of food to help," she said. "You can't ask that of decent people. They won't do it."

Like most pipe smokers, she smokes about 10 percent of the time and spends the rest just playing with the thing. Finally, she lit up.

"But why you?" I asked. "It wasn't your area."

"You can't know about this kind of thing and not do something," she said. "We are part of this world. That makes us responsible."

She seems to have made an art out of coming up with just the right quote. This one was from John Winthrop, one of America's early settlers. "If my neighbor needeth help," she recited, "thou can't not doubt what thou must do."

I asked if Ethiopia was truly our neighbor. Had they not embraced Russia?

It is the children you must look at, she said. A hungry child has no politics.

I had coffee - I was fighting jet lag. She had wine.

I asked her about the day-to-day of her job. It turns out that being an ambassador is not that glamorous. Mostly, it involves sitting through long meetings, pushing for just the right clause in the latest FAO proposal. I told her it sounded dull. She laughed, then came back with one of her favorite phrases.

"It's the only way to get things done," she said.

It's the lesson of Congress, she explained. It's not enough to be right. You must make others believe too.

She is 74. I asked how she felt about her Senate defeat.

"My dear," she said, "I was really looking forward to being there. I adored Congress."

How do you pick yourself up after that kind of disappointment?

"Wednesday morning," she said, "I was absolutely stunned. Thursday, I woke up and said, 'The good Lord knows best. I'm not going to let it get me. Don't look back. Don't waste your time. Look forward.'"

"Still," I said, "a disappointment like that would throw most people."

"Well," she said, "you can't always have life on your own terms. What you have to do is stick to principle, keep pushing for what you believe in."

I asked it a different way - does she miss the fame? She looked out the window a moment. The sun came onto her face. She told me there was an important distinction in the pursuit of career - the difference between getting somewhere and doing something.

"For me," she said, "that difference is everything."

I asked her about the frustration. She has taken on one of the most difficult of issues. Even the optimists say it will be decades before the Third World can feed itself - if ever.

She came up with a quote from a rabbi she had known. "You will never arrive at the solution," he told her. "You will never be absolved of the responsibility of trying."

She asked the waiter for espresso. There would be meetings until evening and she needed to be sharp.

"Success isn't the measure of a human being," she said. "Effort is. What are you trying to do?"

Her pipe went out. She played with it for a few minutes, then touched a match to the bowl. I noticed that she inhaled the smoke. This is going to sound sexist, but it's part of understanding what she's about - until I had lunch with Millicent Fenwick, I would have never believed a woman could smoke a pipe and still look so damned feminine.

I asked how long she plans to stay at it. She told me of how she often dreams of her home in New Jersey, the one she grew up in and still owns. She'd also like to have time to garden. And write. And read.

I thought this was a buildup to saying she'd done her time. Put in two years. She would be heading back soon. Instead, she said it could be a while - maybe years more. There's still a lot to be done.

"It's a terribly complex problem," she said, "but it would be lovely to think I've helped just a little bit."

I suppose most public figures are drawn to the great headline-making issues. Millicent Fenwick has chosen instead to embrace the desperately poor in countries most Americans have never heard of.

Two choices: getting somewhere or doing something. I think, between the two, I know which is a greater measure of belief. ■■

Tuesday, December 11, 1984

▼

ADDIS ABABA, Ethiopia - I am watching men from Britain load food from Australia onto American planes bound for hungry nomads in this socialist land.

Nearby, I watch a few dozen Russians do the same. There are reports that Cubans have been helping them. Italians are also here. And Germans. French, too. And, of course, the United States.

There is a hopeful side to the suffering of a people. When it is big enough, it is a magnet to the compassion of nations.

In 30 minutes, I am to leave for one of the camps.

At the moment, I am sitting in the tent of the British Royal Air Force. They are an imposing bunch, given to cycle gang mustaches and tattooed forearms. Were you to see them on a dark night, you would cross the street. Almost all volunteered to give up Christmas to fly food to Ethiopian children.

When I first called them, I told the lieutenant I wanted to write of his crew as unsung heroes, men as crucial to saving lives as the doctors in the field. Most people eat up that kind of pitch. Pilots are different.

"Skip the flattery, mate," said the lieutenant. "If we're flying, you've got a ride. Good enough?"

They usually get up at 4:30 in the morning, fly eight runs a day, load the holds themselves and land on strips so treacherous they've had to cut tire pressure to absorb the rocks. They are 4,000 miles from their families. Their airfield accommodations are a tent. They say they have never had a better assignment.

"You figure you may be doing a bit of good," one crewman explained.

They have been called the feed-the-hungry version of the French Foreign Legion. The only thing that angers them is not having supplies for a run. They hate days off.

I arrive at their tent at 6:10. Most are already here. I watch one of the more burly ones heft food crates from truck to plane. His name is Derek Barron.

"Miss home?" I ask.

"Matter of fact," he says, "my wife just had a baby."

I ask when.

"Two days after I got here."

Why did he volunteer if he knew he was about to become a father? He says that is why. Makes you think about kids, he says.

I ask about his previous assignments. He mentions he was in the Falklands war. He didn't mind what he saw there, but he's made a point of avoiding the feeding camps of Ethiopia. The airstrips are as far as he goes. War, he can handle. Starving children he could not do.

It is not just a coming together of nations. It is religions, too.

Catholic Relief is here, and so are the Christians of World Vision. The Lutherans are here, the Jesuits too, and today, ready to board the plane, is a man named Barry Weiss of a New York Jewish agency.

"Why are you guys here?" I ask Weiss.

"Hunger," he says. "It's a humanitarian issue."

Many of the people they are helping to feed are Moslems.

One world.

I decide to try speaking to the Russians. A lineup of Antonov AN-12s sits across the tarmac. It takes me 10 minutes to cross it. I've

Dawn at the airport: Derek Barron of the RAF, an hour before we left for Korem.

▲
9

been told the Ethiopians keep East and West strictly separate. I am surprised to find no guards stopping me.

Soon, I am standing by three Russians, men in their 30s. For a moment, we eye each other uncertainly.

"American journalist," I finally say. "You speak English?"

Two of the three do. They seem uncomfortable, but gracious.

"You've been in the camps?" I ask.

"Yes," one says. "It's very hard, people living that way in this world."

"It's good to see everyone working together," I say.

"Yes," the other one says. "It is good."

We shake hands. I recross the tarmac. At 8:30, I board the Hercules for Alamata, the landing strip closest to Korem, the most difficult camp.

The RAF crew brought sandwiches to get themselves through the day. As soon as we landed, Roger Clements gave them away.

I strap into a paraseat, my knees against seven ton of supply. The captain gets on the intercom to announce we'll be flying somewhere above ground level - his words. Four days after coming here, I am in the air.

I have been on quieter flights. Less bumpy ones, too. The only amenities are airsickness bags. "Actually," says a crewman, "we've been getting some pretty good use out of them lately."

The rougher the flight gets, the more the RAF enjoys it. They are of a mind that commercial pilots are elderly ladies. If your fuselage isn't rattling violently in at least a hundred places, it's not a real airplane. If you're not landing with too heavy a load on too short a strip, you're not earning your check.

A half-hour out, they invite me into the cockpit, where I finally find a window view.

You hear drought, you think desert. It's not that way. Below, the land looks like a hundred Colorados. Big country. The peaks reach 11,000 feet.

The copilot points to the left. "That's how bad conditions are," he says.

He is speaking of an impressive river, strong enough over the centuries to have cut canyon through mountain. Its banks are wide. Its trough is deep. It is completely dry. I have never seen a riverbed like this without water. As I stare, I find myself hunching into my jacket.

"I didn't think it would be that bad," I say to the copilot.

"It gets worse further north," he says.

We talk for a few minutes. I ask if he's seen the camps.

"Unfortunately not," he says.

"Why's that unfortunate?"

"People should see things like that."

The touchdown in Alamata is jarring, but done perfectly. I step out of the plane. A sudden shadow comes over me. I look up for the cloud. It is not a cloud. The runway, beat dry by the bad years, has kicked up enough dust to shroud the sun.

Then I see the children. There are a scattering of thatch huts by the runway. The children come timidly forward. I have never seen children so thin.

They reach out, as do their parents, and what looks like grandparents. I stand with my palms up. I have nothing for them. If these are the conditions of people surviving on their own, I cannot imagine what the camps must be like.

Behind me, I hear footsteps. Roger Clements, the RAF loadmaster, is carrying an armful of sandwiches the crew had taken to get through the day. He hands them to the families. He speaks quietly to himself as he walks away.

"For bloody sake," he says. "We don't need 'em."

We have luck. A beat-up vehicle bound for Korem is waiting for some of the other passengers. There is room.

Slowly, the car grinds clockwise uphill, 10 to 15 miles an hour. It is a bad road, but it is road. The turns are blind. Our left wheels are often 18 inches from a thousand-foot drop.

One kind of tree seems to have survived the drought. Someone in the car tells me they are acacias.

"Pretty sturdy," I say.

"Yes," he says. "But a little further, the cactus are dying."

I have never heard of hot weather killing cactus before. The land has turned against more than just the people.

In one hour, I will be in the camp. ■■■

Wednesday, December 12, 1984

KOREM, Ethiopia - The first thing that struck me was the sound. Except it was not sound. It was the absence of sound. People everywhere, and so little sound. Starvation does make a noise. It is silence. And it is very loud.

Then I noticed the flies. They covered the eyes of the weaker children. And the weaker men, too, and the weaker women. I once worked on a farm. The flies on the cattle were not as bad as the flies I saw now.

Thousands of people. Tens of thousands. The fortunate few live in sheds. The fortunate many live in pits of dirt covered by plastic.

The rest - more than 15,000 - live on the ground, measuring wealth by that one possession most treasured here: a blanket.

There are blankets for only a few. Each serves a family of four, sometimes more. At dusk, they huddle beneath them, and each morning, perhaps 20 families wake to find one of their number no longer alive. It is the paradox of drought country that here, where the sun has become such an enemy, it is the cold, at night, that does much of the killing.

Five thousand straw tepees stretch toward the mountains. Three thousand plastic tent shrouds stretch toward the town. Up to 20 people are packed beneath each.

Wandering souls cover the rest of this ground, as dense as a crowd at a stadium. It can take five minutes to move 10 yards. Most are so thin they don't even show muscle. It has been consumed by the body.

Truly, I have arrived in Korem.

Before I left America, I wondered how this could go on. How long can it take to master a refugee problem? Now I understood. Even a nation of resources would find it hard to serve 55,000 suddenly destitute people - even if they had appeared near a city. But these people are not near a city, they are in mountains difficult to reach. And Ethiopia has few resources, few planes, few trucks.

Nor are there just these 55,000. There are other camps, other refugees. Throughout the north country, and some of the south, there are hundreds of thousands more, all having clung to their mountain homes until this last failed harvest left them starving, finally leaving, streaming for hope, walking for days, arriving near death at camps unable to handle those already there. And still, every day, more people arrive than supplies.

There is only one force in this place that is stronger than the pain. A surprising humanity.

It is a nearly impossible humanity. Shipments of wheat will come into Korem. They will be placed on the open ground. People will gather around - people quite literally starving. People so hungry they think only of their hunger. People perhaps days from death. And they will not touch the wheat.

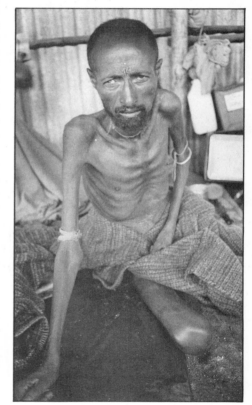

They will sit nearby, waiting patiently, sometimes for hours, sometimes more than a day.

Several times, trucks filled with food have broken down enroute to Korem. It is the same road the newest refugees travel on their journey to the camp. And never once have they touched the trucks, even those left unguarded. That would be stealing. That would be wrong. So they continue walking.

An Ethiopian named Simachew, fluent in English, is the supervisor of the camp. He tells me there are two days of food left, with supplies down to a trickle. The weaker children weigh half what they should. The day before I arrived, they ran out of dry milk. Even if it comes, it will solve little.

They need wood to boil it. And there is not enough wood.

I saw him in the hospital in Korem. I wish I could say he was one of the worst cases. He was not.

There is not enough medicine, either. Or enough plastic for more tents.

Nor enough stretchers, making it difficult to transport the dead.

I walk outside, stopping at a waiting place for the sick, one of many. A child next to me is crying. He reaches up, I reach down. He encircles his fist around my finger and the crying stops. He encircles his arms around my leg. He will not let go. So, together, like that, we stand for five minutes.

I walk again, and the children gather, as they had in the Addis Ababa ghetto, only more of them, hundreds of them. All reach for me. I was told to try not to touch, there is much disease here. But I have nothing else for them, and touching seems to be a medicine, so I give them my hands.

All have the same name for me. Ferengee. Foreigner. From their lips, it sounds less like a greeting than a prayer. When I look at them, they each make the same gesture. They draw a line across one palm with the other hand, then pat their chests thrice. "Ferengee," they say again. In the future, whenever a child touches my hand, I think I will remember Korem.

At first, I did not use my camera. It seemed more than an intrusion. Then they began pointing to it. They wanted photographs taken. It had nothing to do with vanity, of course. They understood something even many Americans do not, that help can come through lenses.

"They know," said Mr. Simachew. "They understand the world is trying to share their problems."

He has heard people say it: Foreigners are coming to help us. Americans especially.

Nearby, I spot a child picking slivers off the ground, bringing them to his mouth. I cannot imagine what he could be eating. The earth is hard and cracked, the mosaic of a broken windshield. I bend to take the child's picture. I shoot for three minutes. When I look up, I am in shadow.

Maybe two hundred people are gathered around me. As I stand, they chant their prayer. Ferengee.

That night, I found a room in the nearby town for one dollar. The floor was concrete, the ceiling corrugated steel. It contained a bed

This is how the luckier people of Korem lived. The less fortunate slept outside, without blankets.

and nothing else. The hallway was dirt. There was no water or electricity. A cold I did not expect settled onto the mountains. I slept in a flannel shirt, huddling beneath the covers, and still, I found myself shivering. I wondered how those in the fields, without blankets, could endure this. Soon, I would see.

At dawn, a thousand roosters woke the town. By 6:30, I was heading back to the camp with three of the young French doctors who work there. Morning in Korem, the worst time.

The mist is beautiful. We stop the truck by a section of tents. Nearby, three men are dismantling a thatch tepee.

"One of the people inside must have died," says the doctor I am with. I ask how he knows. He explains that it has become custom to use tepee poles as slings.

In another tent, a second child has died. Weak first from hunger, then disease, the night cold finally took him. I do not want to look in. Then I decide I should. I did not come here to look away.

The child lies half-covered. He was very young. He is horribly thin. The family has begun a ritual washing.

All around me, a wail begins to spread. There is certainly no wealth here, or possessions, or food, but there is community. One family's loss becomes the loss of all families, and all join in the mourning. The men cry, too.

We walk toward the morgue.

"Twenty-one so far," says the man outside it.

Nearby, 50 people sit vigil. All are wailing softly.

It is mourning, but more than mourning. It sounds like fear, too - perhaps of the pain they know this will bring. As I leave, the wail gets louder. I do not look back.

We walk on, into one of the hospital units. I pause by a father and son. The son lies in the father's arms. The father calls softly to the son.

I turn to the doctor. "That child looks bad," I say.

The doctor bends over for a closer look. "He died during the night," he says.

Back outside, the sun hits the mountains with a beauty that makes me stop and stare. We move toward the more hopeful side of the camp. A hundred fires are going. The day's cooking has begun, with the last of the wood. This is not a secret place. The whole camp knows this is where the limited food supply is prepared. And no one bothers it.

"I still find that hard to understand," says the doctor.

He has long since been able to pull the curtain down to the tragedies of this place. The one thing he still cannot get used to is the decency.

On our way out, we pass lines for everything. Water, medical help, food, of course. The lines stretch hours long.

No one complains. No one jostles.

The people crowd around as we climb into the car. They smile and reach out.

"Ferengee," they say.

Other than that, there is no sound.

We drive away in silence. I look back, watching them begin their day: 55,000 of the most desperate of people, living in near-impossible conditions.

And it occurs to me that there are no police in this city of refugees. And no crime.

I had never before been to a place so inhuman. Or more civilized. ■■■

Like many at Korem, these women posed willingly. They wanted the world to know.

Thursday, December 13, 1984

KOREM, Ethiopia - I'd heard about her in Addis Ababa. Small legends emerge in famine country, and she is one of them, the senior doctor in Ethiopia's biggest feeding camp.

I met her during my second hour here, which to me was a long time in this place. She has been here seven months. She is 32 and from France. Her name is Brigitte Vasset.

In Korem, every day, she tends over a hundred patients, only not like most patients - these are all critical. Nor are they her only concern. Always, at the door of the hospital, a thousand more wait for her. And there are more still, uncounted numbers who reach for her, pleading, wherever she walks.

The word hospital implies a building. In Korem, it is not that way. It is more a depository, a long shed with dirt floor. The patients lie on foot-high platforms built of rock and mud. The platforms are the size of an average bed. Four people are squeezed onto each.

I follow her inside, into the isolation section, where she kneels to touch a woman's abdomen, searching for an enlarged spleen, a sign of a disease called relapsing fever. It can push your temperature to 104.

I ask her how it's transmitted.

"By lice," she says.

"Aren't you risking exposure yourself?"

"I've already had it," she says, "so I'm okay."

She explains that she gets a lot of things from her patients. It's all right, she says; in a place like this, it's unavoidable. If it's bad, you take a day off. Either way, you get over it.

Her cloak is dirty. Her hair is auburn. She is tall and thin.

I find it hard getting used to her being here. You think of doctors as humanitarians as long as they can have their comfort. There are few medical choices less comfortable than this.

Together, we walk outside, into an extraordinary sight. There are hundreds of some of the sickest people I have ever seen, but not sick enough to get into this hospital.

Many show knees that are swollen triple size, expecting her to work some magic. She tells me the knees are not swollen at all. They

are normal. It is the legs that are astonishingly thin.

Vasset pauses as they gather around her.

"These old people," she says. "You leave them outside, they will die."

I ask how she chooses.

"I don't know how we choose," she says. "The oldest one, the weakest one."

"It must be hard."

"It is the hardest part," she says. "But I must."

Most hospitals have more doctors and nurses than patients. Here, it is ten staff members to a thousand.

She mentions the shortage of blankets.

"We only have enough for the weakest patients," she says. "The worst of the children."

I expect her to ask me to stress the need for more. She doesn't. She has come to understand she must work with what she has.

A woman wraps her arms around Vasset's leg. Others reach for her, pulling at her. They are not rough, just desperate. Still, I expect her to get angry at any moment. She is so overwhelmed, so overworked, in such a hurry. And now they are pulling at her.

She does not get angry. She kneels and touches the face of the woman holding her leg.

"Mama," Vasset says softly. "Oh, mama."

She moves to another unit where three new patients await admission. They are shockingly thin. She examines all three, then turns to an aide.

"Starvation, starvation and starvation," she says. I had not known it was a medical diagnosis.

She moves down the corridor. Those too weak to reach for her draw lines on their palms and pat their chests three times, the sign of need. Flies are everywhere.

She spends an hour going from platform to platform. Soon, she learns there have been two recent deaths. It means two spaces have opened up.

We walk outside. It is the moment of selection. The people can tell by her face that she is about to choose.

I could not do this job. I could not pick

one of a hundred, of a thousand, and leave the others to wail. I could not do that.

She scans the crowd, examines some, then does it quickly.

"Come, mama," she says. "And mama, yes, mama, too."

The two women move slowly inside. Vasset helps them.

"Others are so sick, too," she says. "But there is only room for these."

As she turns to go back, an elderly woman touches her forehead to Vasset's hand, holding tight.

"Mama," says Vasset, and then places her hand around the woman's upper arm. Vasset does not have big hands, but she is still able to encircle the arm, touching her right thumb against her right forefinger.

I have never seen anyone do that. How could any adult be so thin?

"It's all right, mama," Vasset says, and rejects her.

"She is not so bad," she tells me as we walk inside. She pauses to demonstrate on an in-patient, again encircling the upper arm, only this time there is much room to spare.

It is the dirtiest medical area I have ever seen. It is extraordinary that they're able to keep it this clean.

Again, she kneels on the floor. She begins to examine a very old woman who sits by a younger one. She looks into her eyes.

"The grandmother?" I ask.

"This one is not so old," she says.

I ask how old the patient is.

"Twenty," the patient says.

Vasset looks surprised.

"I would have said 25," she says. She is used to this.

I try talking as she works.

"How do you get to them all?" I ask.

"It is better," she says. "Once, we had 200 patients each. Today, it's 100."

She explains that there are now five doctors. Five doctors, 55,000 people.

"It doesn't sound like a lot," I say.

"This is how I measure," she says. "Two months ago, 100 died each day. This morning, only 23."

Patients aren't the only ones who pull at her. Aides do, too. And nurses. And other doctors. At every moment, she is talking to

Brigitte Vasset, Korem's senior doctor. She had thousands of patients, a deep fatigue and endless commitment.

three people. There is no such thing as five minutes to rest. Not even one.

"I don't know how you've kept up for seven months," I say.

She smiles, explaining that she's spent four years in places like this, most recently Afghanistan and Chad.

I ask when she plans to go home.

"Not yet."

"Why not?"

Again the smile, and for the first time, she looks square at me.

"I like this place," she says. "I like these people."

I try asking about her motivation. I wait for her to tell me about commitment to the Third World. She doesn't. Her calling is medicine, not philosophy.

It's quite simple, she says. She is a doctor. There is healing to be done here.

"You have family back in France?" I ask.

"Oh yes."

"When did you last get to see them?"

"A long time ago."

"What about personal life?"

"I get off at 6," she says. "I eat. I fall asleep. It's enough."

"And your pay for all this?"

She says it is four hundred dollars.

Per week?

"Per month."

She continues her rounds, stopping suddenly to stare at a bed.

She lifts the cover, scanning the patients underneath.

"We have a place," she says. "There are only three on this bed."

Immediately, she walks outside and selects another. For her, it is a victory.

I find it hard to see. Every morning, up to 150 new patients join the thousand already at the door. Every day, more come from the hills into the camp.

She does not think of those things. She looks not for solutions, just for signs of small gain.

She asks me only one favor. Leave her name out if I want to, she says, but please, could I mention her organization? It is called Doctors Without Borders. It places doctors like her wherever there are places like this.

I'd begun to feel guilty about taking her time. I told her I'd let her go.

I shook her hand, then watched her move back down the dirt floor, a very bright light in a very dark room. ■■■

The hospital beds were made of rock and mud. Four people slept on each one.

Friday, December 14, 1984 ▼

KOREM, Ethiopia - It was almost night, which falls early in this place. There is no electricity to hold it back. Three of us sat against the stone-wall building where the Westerners stay. About 10 live here, mostly medical people. They're all about 30. Most left their lives months ago to work the camp before it was news. Most plan to stay for months more.

The two I was with were women. Both smoked cigarettes. Every Westerner who works in Korem smokes cigarettes.

"It's funny," said Kathy Bogan. "When we go home, we stop, but here, you fall back into it."

She's a nutritionist from England. Her job is to feed 10,000 children a day.

I was off in my own thoughts.

"What do you do to make it stop at night?" I asked.

"You just get used to it," she said.

More than 20 children die in Korem each day. I asked Kathy if she's lost any she's grown close to. She said the orphans can be hard. The Westerners tend to make the orphans their own.

"We name them after our staff," she said. "David Alexander died last week. Tony Nash died the week before."

She stood and excused herself. She and the doctors had planned a meeting to discuss the new food shortage. The food had stopped coming.

I was left alone with Ita Reilley, a children's nurse, also from England, here to open a new camp farther north. She has spent much of her time in this kind of work.

"Does it harden you?" I asked.

"Quite a bit," she said.

I asked if that wasn't bad.

"No," she said. "It's good. You have to be able to do the job. If it got to you, you couldn't do it."

I stared up for a time. I've seen few skies as good as the night sky of Ethiopia.

As a child, she went to private school. Now, the closest hot shower is five hours by car. The closest phone is an hour. There is no nightlife, no TV, no movies, no newspapers. I

told her it must feel good to get back to London.

"Yes," she said, "but not for too long."

"Don't you like home?"

"I do," she said. "It's just that as soon as you hear things are getting bad somewhere, like Ethiopia, you want to do something about it."

She lighted another cigarette. I asked if she doesn't get a twinge on holidays.

"A little," she said. "You always make a phone call, if there's a phone. Say hello. But your life's out here."

I couldn't see her face anymore. Dusk had gone to night. I could hear the doctors discussing the food problem, but could not see them, either.

We sat without talking for a few minutes. Then she volunteered something.

"Every time I head back here," she said, "my friends all say, 'You're mad.'"

"So why do you?"

"I don't know. Because it's what I do. Because there's still suffering."

She is 29. I asked how much longer she planned to do this work.

Kathy Bogan, of Save The Children, worked as a camp nutritionist. Like all Westerners in Africa, she seemed always to be smoking.

▲
17

"I used to say until I was 30," she said. "But I have a few friends in it who said the same thing, and they seem to go on. Thirty-five, more."

She was not the type to talk about herself. None of them are. But slowly, she dropped her reserve.

"Most of my friends have settled down," she said. "Gotten married. I suppose I'd like children, too."

"So why not just go back and see what happens?"

For Ita Reilly, and her colleagues, this, they said, is what it was about - the children.

She shrugged. "Hard to say. You know how people are. They have things they have to do."

I told her it's not as if she hadn't put in her time.

It took her a few seconds to answer.

"Maybe I can put in a little more," she said.

I asked what she does with her leisure. It seemed to be one advantage of working these camps. You appreciate your time off.

"Oh," she said. "Usually I'll just read a book. When there's electricity. Or get up late. There's really not much else."

"Doesn't sound like a lot," I said.

"Well," she said, "we listen to music, too." I could hear a smile in her voice. "We all have our Sony Walkmen. Those are important."

She makes $7,000 a year. Like many Westerners in Africa's remote areas, she often gets sick. I asked what she hopes to achieve here.

She told me of a moment during the afternoon. Two children arrived at the camp in appalling condition. Because of the thousands of others, they might have had to wait a day to register for food. Ita happened to see them, though.

She stopped what she was doing, and made sure they were fed immediately.

Little things, she said, and then, matter-of-factly: "It's not so much to ask to have a full belly, is it?"

In one of the nearby huts, I could see a fire. Dogs barked in the distance. I kept thinking about the number of people in the camp.

"It's so big," I finally said. "Don't you ever think you're barely making a dent?"

"All the time," she said. "But if a thousand die, and you've saved a hundred, or ten, or even one, well, you've done a little bit."

She planned to leave the next day to start the new camp. She could not have picked a more difficult job. New camps, for a time, are the worst of all camps. It takes time to get organized. Word spreads of such a place, and always, in the first weeks, there is a deluge. You can't keep up with it.

Neither of us said anything for a few minutes. Then, for the second time, she offered something on her own.

"These people have a right to live, you know," she said. "And they're not asking very much. They're not asking for anything at all, really."

We could hear the others putting dinner together. She said she wasn't hungry. She had things to think about.

I walked away, leaving her there alone. An hour later, I glanced over, and she was still there, her cigarette glowing in the dark. ■■■

Sunday, December 16, 1984

KOREM, Ethiopia - It had always been difficult land, but it was his land, as it had been his father's and his grandfather's. So, four harvests ago, when the rains did not come, he saw it not as an omen, just as a bad year. There had been other bad years. There was no reason to think of leaving. This mountain was his home.

He was telling me this in the Korem camp, which is where he now lives. It is also where his son is buried. There are 55,000 people here, but really only one story. Any farmer, anywhere, broken by weather, knows it. This farmer's name was Badassie. His wife, Fatuma, sat beside him. She was very beautiful, although weak from hunger.

The camp supervisor, Mr. Simachew, did the translating.

During the good years, his life took on the rhythm of the land. He would sow in April and harvest in November, always corn, wheat and sorghum. He was a good farmer, harvesting enough to market.

They ate meat in those days, big meals, like Americans eat, often throwing out what was left over.

He even had oxen, four of them, and he grew to see them as a farmer often sees his animals, like sons. He named one of them Strong, one Black, one Red, and the last In-between. Sometimes he'd bring them food from his table. Those were the fat years.

Then a child came, a son. They were a family now. Soon, the boy began to talk and there was little quiet around the house.

Evenings, the family would take walks along the land. They saw it like a mother, fertile, a source of life.

That was the year the rains stopped coming. Slowly, the young crop withered. The corn turned brown, the wheat burnt. Badassie waited until late November and still harvested only a little. But he told himself a farmer is a farmer. He bends with the weather. Next year, it would turn.

A second son came and, once again, the rains did not. But the child made their place here more rooted. Now two had been born of this land. The young son became special, as youngest children often do.

Even before the child could talk, the father found himself bending over him at night, telling him what he would inherit when he was a man, the oxen, the land, these mountains. What is mine will be yours.

By now, into the second year of drought, the land was no longer like a mother; it had turned dry and resistant. Still, Badassie sowed his crop.

Farmers, he knew, must be gamblers. True, the land was now not fertile, but the rain would soon make it so. It was his wager.

But again the rains did not come. Now, every day, he would poke through the ground, looking for shoots. None emerged. None at all. In November there was no harvest.

That year, the food began to run out. There was no more meat, no more vegetables.

But even as the land dried out, he vowed to hold to it, as his father had, and his grandfather. They had made the land work. He would, too.

So he made the hard decision. First he sold his furniture. Then his farm implements. Then the donkeys. And eventually, when his sons grew thinner than he could bear, he sold Black. And Red. Then In-between, and finally, the most loved of them, Strong.

Badassie and Fatuma - one couple, but really every couple. She was too weak to walk. He had to carry her.

19

That was when the first tragedy occurred. It occurred suddenly. They were all weak from a fragile diet, and as happens, the children were weakest.

One day, his eldest boy caught a cold, which normally is nothing, but these times were not normal. Because hunger had taken his strength, the cold turned into pneumonia. And one night, the pneumonia took him.

The father buried the child, and that same day, decided it would only harden his resolve.

His place was here. Land does not turn against you, the weather does, and this land was his. It was hard land, but striking land. Live among the mountains long enough, and they become part of you. The land was his soul.

Now he would sit up at night, holding his youngest, telling him the time of pain was over. He would make promises.

For you, things will be different, he would say. When a family takes a stand, even weather can be beaten. And they would make a stand.

Every day he watched the sky. Occasionally clouds came, bringing hope, but they passed as quickly. And again the rains failed. This time, even the pasture weeds died.

Cows died, too. The money for meat had long since gone, now there was no money for bread either. Or wheat. And even if there had been, there was no wheat.

Amongst themselves, the men began to talk. Perhaps we should go.

But where?

Anywhere; there's nothing left here.

But it's all we know. And rain is due, long due.

But children are starving.

" But again the rains did not come. Now, every day, he would poke through the ground, looking for shoots. None emerged. None at all."

Yes, but surviving. We're still surviving.

One day, as the men agonized, word came to town about a shelter beyond the mountains. In Korem. There was food there. Food from America. It was enough to draw the most desperate. Slowly, in a trickle, the town began to empty.

But he resisted. He had promised his boy so much. They were impovershed now, but leaving would impoversh them forever. He would not do that. He was a man, he would provide.

He began to wander the fields, scratching the ground, finding the merest bits of sorghum, bringing them to his wife, who made it into soup, though it was really more water than soup.

And then it touched him again. Illness came to the daughter of his brother. Weakened by hunger, she could not hold. His family was a close one, and a death for one was a shared loss, belonging to all. It was as if the daughter had been his own. And finally, he understood.

The land could go. All of it could go. But not his son. His son he had to protect.

The next day, the three of them left for Korem. Before setting out, he knelt on his land, placing his palms against it. It was still his land. His soul. He had no anger at it. Just pain.

The walk took four days. There was no food. And then it happened.

His boy began to fail. They had all grown so thin, so gradually, that he'd lost sight of what starvation looked like. Now he saw it had been happening to his son.

There was nothing but leaves, so he tried to feed him leaves. There was no hope but in this journey, so they tried to walk faster. But the sun and the mountains were hard.

And at night, the cold settled down, and his son weakened, and weakened more. And by the time they made Korem, two weeks ago, the son had entered that difficult phase, so hungry he could no longer eat.

He died on the third day. The father's new neighbors, living nearby in Korem's open field, mourned with him, then offered to help carry the child to the morgue. The father asked if he could first have a moment.

He held the boy close, and out loud, he said goodbye.

Ethiopians are people of dignity. The father did not cry once during the telling of this story. Afterward, he and his wife willingly posed for a photograph. Then they walked back toward the field where they were to sleep.

I looked down at my camera. It was for only a moment, but when I looked up, I could not pick them out. They were lost among the thousands like them. ▪▪▪

Monday, December 17, 1984

▼

ADDIS ABABA, Ethiopia - I had one more hour in Korem. Breakfast was at 7:30. And among the relief workers, as always, the talk was about the children. What to do about the milk shortage? The hygiene problem? The new ones coming in? What to do about the children?

Certainly, there are more adults in this feeding camp, and as much compassion for them. But if you listen close, there is an obsession here with children.

Six of us climbed into the truck. We headed down the mountain. The villages we passed all seemed to be bustling. I said it was good to see people here getting by on their own. Kathy Bogan, a Korem nutritionist, was in the truck with us.

"They're all looking for food," she said.

"To buy?" I asked.

"No," she said, "they're hoping to register with the government for distribution."

I told her I'd thought it was just the camp. "No," she said, "it's all around here. There's no food anywhere."

We made it to the strip at 9, the same one we'd landed on, a dirt run standing alone, surrounded by parched field.

Like most air travel from the north country, it was blind gamble. You don't call the ticket counter for flight times. You show up, sit under the sun and hope something with room shows up.

We had to wait only an hour. Someone pointed to a buzzing speck above the mountains. We shielded our eyes and watched it come in. It turned out to be the deHavilland Twin Otter run by World Vision. It's been flying famine missions here for three years, the crews sometimes doing 12 months' duty.

We flew out of the valley, back over the dry river. Funny things come to mind when you're leaving a place like this. I found myself thinking about the camp's starving girls and women. Almost all wore earrings.

We touched down in Kombulcha, the stopping point for Bati, one of the harder camps. One man got off the plane. I'd originally planned to go myself.

The pilot looked back at me. I shook my head. You can only see so much.

The hopeful side of Korem - the feeding center. I found its pediatrician, Dr. Azeb Tamrat, with her children.

▲

21

As we sped for takeoff, I noticed a stack of Canadian wheat. Nearby, there was a helicopter preparing to fly it in. The helicopter was Russian.

An hour later, we were in Addis. I climbed down to the tarmac and spotted one of the crew. His shirt tag said Keith Ketchum. He said he'd been flying here for 10 months. I asked him why.

He gave the answer you often hear from people of his faith - because he's a Christian. Then he said something you don't hear as often. "It's fine to go around saying you love the Lord, and all that," he said, "but I think you gotta do something about it, too,"

How did seeing Korem change me? I wasn't sure at first. When I was in the middle of it, taking notes, taking pictures, I'd pulled the curtain down pretty good. I mentioned that to one of the nurses there. She said she'd been able to do the same thing when she first came, but found it doesn't work that way.

It'll tell, she said. You can shut things off at the time, but you can't expect to be done with them.

I got back to the hotel around 1 p.m. I wasn't at all tired. I'd gotten a better sleep in my dollar-fifty room in Korem than I had in the Hilton. I decided to take a quick shower and start writing. I turned on the water and then just stood there. For 10 minutes, 20, finally more than an hour. I can't remember ever taking that long a shower.

Afterward, at about 2, I lay down for a moment. When I opened my eyes, it was 9 p.m. I've never been a napper. It was the first time I'd slept like that during the day in 10 years.

When I'd first gotten to Korem, I'd heard

" The first thing I noticed was the sound. There was sound here. Almost too much sound. I don't know how they did it, but they'd made these children healthy again".

---

they had a feeding center just for children, 10,000 of them. I didn't think I wanted to see it. The main camp was hard enough. But in the end, I did go. I sturdied myself as the truck pulled up. I figured this would be the worst of it.

It was the opposite.

The first thing I noticed was the sound. There was sound here. Almost too much sound. I don't know how they did it, but they'd made these children healthy again. I could not get used to this: Hope in Korem.

It took me 10 minutes to make my way to her side. Her name was Dr. Azeb Tamrat. She is the pediatrician here, an Ethiopian fluent in English.

I tried asking her a question but was drowned out. I was getting what is known here as the welcome - 5,000 kids shouting the word ferengee, for foreigner, over and over. I felt like I was running for something.

The doctor laughed, then gestured toward the bigger camp.

"You go down there," she said, "you cannot smile. Here, you can smile."

Children, everywhere. When they first came here, she said, most could barely move.

"Bone and skin," she said. "Look at them now. This is what can be done."

I thought back to the sicker ones I'd seen in the main camp. I said I had not thought it was possible to bring them back.

A nutritionist from the center was standing with us. "Children have an incredible will to survive," she said. "More than adults. They fight and fight and fight."

I asked the doctor how she liked it here.

"Well" she said, "I have a seven-month-old baby at home."

"And you left?" I said.

A hundred children crowded around her.

"My child is fine," she said. "He is healthy. I am needed here."

Unconciously, she touched the cheeks of those nearby.

"So these are your children, meanwhile," I said.

"These are the children of everybody," she said.

I am thinking now of a quote from Robert Kennedy. He was once asked how he'd like the first line of his obituary to read. This is what he said: "I think again back to what Camus wrote about the fact that perhaps this world is a world in which children suffer, but we can lessen the number of suffering children, and if you do not do this, then who will do this? I'd like to feel that I'd done something to lessen that suffering."

I'm not sure whether I believe in an afterlife, whether a man's spirit lives on. Having been to Korem, I believe it a little more. ■

Tuesday, December 18, 1984

KHARTOUM, Sudan - The first hour I was here, I thought the desert had taken this place. There was sand outside the airport, sand throughout downtown, sand everywhere. When you breathed, you inhaled sand.

It was not the desert after all. It was drought. Not long ago, Khartoum was green. Drought has baked it into dust.

I came here because I heard the drought was not just in Ethiopia. It is true. More than 600 miles from Addis Ababa, the weather is maiming another civilization.

Of every city I know, Khartoum is the last place I'd want to stay, or even stop. The traffic is terrible, the phones don't work, the summers are 130 degrees and Islamic law has cleared liquor from the shelves. Now, in the countryside, the food is running out and most rivers are dry. The soil is parched and the animals are dying.

There are places in this world where the problems are so fierce, the living so harsh, you'd think only those with native roots would want to take them on. I could not imagine any soul coming here who did not have to.

I found him in a house on a dusty street by the airport. His name is Jim Geenen. He is from Wisconsin and looks more like a frat brother than a missionary, though I guess he's a little of both. What he does in the Sudan is a symbol of what I was finding in Africa: the most unlikely of American groups helping unknown peasants in the most foreign of soil.

His home office is 7,000 miles away, in Warwick, R.I. It's called the Foster Parents Plan, but has little to do with that. Their mission is to look for the most damned corners of the Third World and send in the expertise to help make them good again. This year, they will spend $2 million in the Sudan. Geenen runs this show for them. He's looking at a stay of two years or more.

I expected him to be a religious type. That would explain it. He isn't, really. He's a former football jock from Wisconsin. I asked why he came here. He shrugged.

"I dunno," he said. "Just trying to make the desert bloom, I guess."

He seems to have two priorities in life

these days, beer and the Sudan. He can't get one; he hopes to help turn the other.

Only one thing makes him truly angry: seeing greenery disappear. It's the last wall against the desert, he explains. He does not want to lose to the desert. He hates to lose. Every time a goat eats a plant here, James Geenen, of Wisconsin, takes it personally.

"Goats," he says. "If I had my way. . . ." He completes the sentence by drawing a finger across his throat. Geenen hates goats.

He wants to show me what he is trying to do. We begin driving out of Khartoum. He's been in the Sudan several months but still talks Midwest American. A motorist edges past us in an intersection.

"Take it, Jack," says Geenen.

Soon, we leave the dust of the city for a dust that is just dust. Everywhere I look, fields of dust, stretching into mirage. This land has truly been damned.

"So why do you call it Foster Parents?" I ask. He explains it's what they did after World War II. It seemed to be the need back then. The need in the 1980s is Third World development, so that is what they do now.

We turn onto a vast sand plain, heading toward the Nile. I have never seen the Nile be-

The land of Sudan looked impossible to me. Jim Geenen knelt upon it and vowed to make it green.

fore. We pull up near the shore. It's an impressive sight, though these days, I understand, it isn't much.

"Lowest point since 1903," says Geenen.

We get out of the car. Proudly, he points west. I see nothing but dust and thornbush.

"So why are we standing in the middle of this desert?" I say.

He looks hurt. "This isn't desert," he says. "We're going to make this grow."

"This?" I say.

This dust is his latest agricultural project. It looks to me as though you'd have better luck planting seeds in plaster.

"Maybe with enough rain," I say.

He shakes his head.

"I don't expect it to rain," he says. "We're going to make it grow without rain."

He leads me toward a rusted pipe, rising from the Nile. He points to it as if it's the Hope Diamond.

"Irrigation pipe," he says.

I guess I don't know much about irrigation, but I've seen soil and I've seen soil. This was not soil.

I ask if he really thinks water will be enough.

"Give me three weeks," he says. "This is going to be green. I'll send you pictures."

"You're an optimist," I say.

"Better stay away from this business if you're not," he says.

He has projects like this in 100 villages. Irrigation, wells, chickens, health centers. Every so often, Geenen finds himself swinging a shovel at a latrine. It does not sound like glamorous work.

"It's not," he says. "Just simple things - but the difference between surviving out here and not surviving."

He says that's all he wants to do. Help the people survive.

"You don't have to do this," I say. "They're not your people."

I notice he is wearing a flannel shirt in the noonday heat. Wisconsin habits die hard. The strange part is he is not sweating. Some people adapt.

"I dunno," he says. "I guess I don't see nationality as a guideline of who should get our help."

We continue driving. There aren't really villages here, rather a latticework of huts connected not by road but dust plain. Every 15 minutes, we stop to see one of his projects. A well, a school, a tree nursery. He is especially big on trees.

Drought is not just weather, it is also the chipping away at vegetation. It is people cutting brush for wood, the sand moving into the open spaces, the desert winning a little more. Geenen hates seeing the desert win. He will fight back with his tree nursery.

He began as many of them do, with the Peace Corps. He came home, saw what was here, remembered what was there and felt a debt. It's how it happens to most of them.

I look around as we drive. There seem to be no people. I ask where they are.

"There are a few," he says, "but almost all are women and children."

"Where are the men?"

"The city," he says. "Looking for work. Day laborers, that kind of thing."

He seems angry at the thought of it.

"It shouldn't be," he says, mostly to himself. I ask what he means.

"It's no life for them. Farmers are what they are."

I still don't know where he draws such kinship for people he's known only a few months.

"Maybe they'll find something in the city," I say.

"There's no hope in the city," he says. "No jobs, nothing. They're meant to be on the land. They were born here. Grandparents died here. It's what they know. It's what they are."

I was beginning to understand Jim Geenen. Somehow, he has grown to love these people. He loves their dignity, their simplicity. He will not allow the weather to destroy them.

We get stuck in a sand rut. He kicks in the gas and we go fishtailing in a semi-circle, finally tearing loose. I see a smile on his lips. I pic-

" What he does in the Sudan is a symbol of what I was finding in Africa: the most unlikely of American groups helping unknown peasants in the most foreign of soil."

ture him as a teenager cruising Wisconsin streets in an old Chevy on a Saturday night. Things we all did. Somewhere, though, he managed to pick up a sense of debt rare among Americans.

After an hour, we return to the irrigation pipe. I am exhausted and thirsty. He wants to keep going. Nothing excites this man more than looking at a good well-bore.

I ask him if he has a job philosophy.

"It's mostly technical," he says. "Mastering the skills. But there's some art to it."

The art, he says, lies in the diplomacy of the village.

"Like now," he says.

He looks at the pipe and shakes his head.

"This project should be further along," he says. "I think I'll have to do a little butt-kicking."

He smiles. "That's the art part."

We go to a nearby stand of huts and seek out the villager he has been working with. He is an old man in white robe and skullcap. His hands are the hands of a farmer who is a farmer no more. Big hands, but soft now. There has been so little work.

Geenen begins to get stern with him. The old man reaches out.

"Help us," he says. "The land is very tired."

Geenen takes the old man's hand in his own.

"That's why I'm here," he says.

I watch them standing there by the Nile, a young man from Wisconsin and an old man from the Sudan, in partnership against the weather.

One world.

I doubt Geenen will ever match the bounty of the great American farmers. But I guess the test isn't whether you can bring good crop from good soil. It's whether you can turn dust to green. He is what drought country needs in this time, a defier of weather.

We head back toward the car. I keep thinking how there is so little here. Just sand and dust and heat. Bad traffic, dry rivers, dying animals. And Geenen loves this place. He loves what it might become.

He turns the ignition. He says if he could, he'd buy me a beer. But he can't, so he's going back to work.

Now, a final time, he points out the window.

"Give me two weeks," he says. "You'll get the pictures."

I look at the dust.

"You're serious," I say. "Like cornfields in Iowa?"

"Like cornfields in Iowa."

I will be waiting for his photos. I know they will come soon. ■■■■

Geenen and I stopped in one of his villages.
These are among the children he hoped to help.

▲

25

Wednesday, December 19, 1984

GEDARIF, Sudan - They are strangers on their own planet. Not just landless, but homeless too. Not just homeless, but nationless. I did not think I could capture drought in Africa without seeing refugees. For that, the best place to come is Gedarif.

There are more of them in the Sudan than anywhere else in Africa, over 700,000. The biggest camp is here, two hours by truck from the eastern border.

At 1 p.m., I walk inside. Everyone within these walls is Ethiopian. First they came for politics - their government is a repressive one. Lately it has been for food. It has prompted the United Nations to devise a new category for them - environmental refugees.

As I look around, I expect to find, beneath the pain, the same good spirit I saw in Korem. There is a different feel, though.

In this camp, children do not gather around. The adults hold back, too. There is almost no movement. Something happens to people who are forced across a border.

There are nearly 25,000 in the camp of Gedarif. Almost every hour, more arrive. The villagers call them newcomers. Michael Menning is their shepherd.

He looked tired when I met him. He had spent the day setting up three new camps. There's no room left in the old ones, he explained. And little water. And more newcomers all the time.

The United Nations is the overseer of Gedarif, but Menning is the provider. His contract is public health, which means almost everything - medicine, water, shelter. He grew up in Minnesota and is now the Sudan director of the International Rescue Committee. In the past months he has had to double, then triple his staff.

He looks like an aging radical, which is pretty much what he is - balding and bearded with an outmoded anger at unfairness.

I told him the camp was bad here, but Ethiopia had been worse. He showed me how important it is to look beneath the surface.

"We're on the brink," he said. "What you saw there, it's about to happen here."

There are too many people, he said. There are too few resources. And this month, throughout the Sudan, the crop just failed.

I was beginning to see what my visit here was about. It was not, as I'd thought, a glimpse at a more hopeful camp. It was a step back in time. Gedarif is Ethiopia six months ago.

I'd left Khartoum for the east that morning at 7. The ride took more than six hours. The bus was cramped, the sun hot, the scenery hard on the spirit. First it was dead cows, then dead goats and, finally, something I never thought I'd see. Dead camels. Camels can go 50 days without water.

The camp was 10 minutes outside town. Instead of the tents of Korem, there were small thatch huts. More than 20 people were inside each.

I found my way to what passed as the camp office. Inside, there were several Sudanese. One agreed to be my guide.

Together, we began to walk. Soon, five men came up to us, blankets over their shoulders, sticks in their hands.

"Newcomers," said my guide.

It is how it happens here. The nationless just arrive. I asked how long they'd been walking.

"Two weeks," one said.

I asked where their wives and children were.

They died on the way.

I looked around. For the first time, I noticed the camp was mostly men.

"The strong men come," said the guide. "The women and children, not as far. A hard journey."

Those who die are buried along the way. The men then keep going. There is no choice.

My guide began to tell me numbers. On this day, 250 newcomers. Yesterday, 300. The day before 1,000 came. The border bleeds.

I was there three hours. I saw malnutrition. And desolation. But here, there was not yet the drama of starvation. Or of nations coming to help. On the surface, at the moment, Gedarif is mostly a place of nothingness. It is where the world's newly lost come and wait to be found. It is 25,000 people just waiting. And wondering. And for an afternoon, I wondered with them.

Where do you run if you are an African facing starvation? What choice is it to flee mountain drought for desert? What answer to escape from a place with no food for a place that soon will also have no food? How must it feel to cross a border in search of hope, and find yourself in a country where the camels are dying?

I think I understand why Gedarif was so quiet. I think it is because the people there know. They know it is coming. They are waiting for it to begin.

At dusk, I went back to town. I sat with Menning. The nationless are a kind of specialty of his. A few years ago, it was the boat people in Thailand. Now the problem is in the Sudan.

He came eight months ago, answering the call of crisis long before the world knew one existed. Back then, there were 7,000 in Gedarif. It has since more than tripled.

We were sitting in the dark. There was no electricity.

For an hour, we talked about the mechanics of running a refugee operation. Then he told me about the library. There is a library in the Gedarif camp.

"How do you have time?" I asked. "You're trying to keep people alive."

It was one of two times during our talk that he would smile.

"You got to have culture," he said. "You should visit it. It's the only lending library in eastern Sudan."

There is also a school in Gedarif. They are teaching literacy. They are even teaching accounting.

But he has little hope for the future.

"It's a question of time," he said.

He understands the way these things work. When the crop fails, and the food runs out, it is not enough to simply turn to Western governments. First, there must be publicity. Usually, though, there is only one spotlight, and right now, it is on Ethiopia. There is a difficult pattern to famine relief. The people must start dying before you can start saving them.

He looked at his watch. He said he had work to do. In the morning, they were to begin moving people to the new camps.

We went outside together. I asked what he needed here besides food. He smiled a second time.

"Donations for books," he said.

If there is a strongest impression I brought from Gedarif, it would not be the malnutrition. Or the drought. Or the camp itself. It was the reaction of the Sudanese.

They are among the world's poorest people. They are themselves facing a crisis of food. You'd think such people would spurn any outsider who threatens the little they have. Instead, they have swung wide their doors. That, to me, is the story of Gedarif.

I stood in the camp with my Sudanese guide. We were done with our tour. As we walked out, I looked at the United Nations fact sheet I'd brought with me. More than 700,000 foreigners have come into this country of 22 million. It is as if 7 million had flooded America. I imagined how we would react to that.

I asked the guide why the Sudanese keep accepting them all.

"They are hungry people who come," he said.

"Your people are hungry, too," I said.

"Yes," he said. "There is little food here."

"So why don't you just say, 'Sorry, go back to Ethiopia'?"

"No, no, no," he said. "That is not good. They are our neighbors. They go back, they will die."

"But it's not Sudan's affair," I said.

If someone comes to your door, he said, you must open it. That is all.

I boarded the bus for Khartoum the next morning at 6:30. Soon, we were heading out of town.

And here and there, in clumps of 5 and 10, blankets over their shoulders, sticks in their hands, the day's newcomers were already arriving. ▬

The refugees of Gedarif. To the left, a father and son. The mother died, as many women do, during the walk from Ethiopia.

Thursday, December 20, 1984

KHARTOUM, Sudan - I am writing this at 3 a.m., outside the doors of the city's airport. I am not here at this hour because my plane is late. It is scheduled to leave at 3:25 for Nairobi. It is how they often do it in Africa. It is the continent of the midnight flight. It is no way to live.

As I sit here, on the curb, in near-darkness, I'm feeling that irony of drought country. It seems that the hotter the days, the colder the nights. In America, you don't think of that when you pack for the desert. I could use a down parka. All I have is a sports jacket.

They told me to be here at 1:30. I pushed it a little and made it by 2. The airport was shut down. The man at the door would not let me in.

"My flight, " I said. "Nairobi."

He disappeared and came back five minutes later.

"Late," he said. "Late."

No surprise, I suppose. They say few things leave on time in Africa.

" Africa, so far has been one of the more deepening experiences of my life. It has also been no day at the beach."

"Ethiopian Air's okay," one traveler told me. "Kenya Air could go either way. Be happy you're not on Sudan Air. At the best, they're two or three days late."

The guy at the door told me the plane would be here in an hour or two. Departure time around 6. I decided against going back to the hotel. Too risky. If I missed this flight, the next one to Nairobi would be three days away. Again, I sit on the curb, beginning to understand why the Sudanese so often use a certain word. Inshallah. It is God's will.

Africa, so far has been one of the more deepening experiences of my life. It has also been no day at the beach.

There is, to begin, in every country, the paper chase. In two weeks here, I've had to get more IDs - about 20 - than in 32 years back home. In the Sudan alone, I needed four stamped letters from the Ministry of the Interior and two photo IDs from the Ministry of Information.

It still wasn't enough. At the refugee camp I'd come to see on the eastern border, the soldier in charge scanned my papers and frowned. Sorry, he said. I couldn't take pictures. In triumph, I showed him my government-stamped photo permission card. He shook his head again. I needed another, he said, a letter specifically entitling me to shoot pictures that day. I smiled and told him he was 100 percent right. It is one of the basic rules of Africa. Always agree with men who carry machine guns.

It is now 5:30 a.m., a half-hour before postponed departure time. Just as hypothermia's sitting in, they open the airport doors. By now, a hundred others have shown up. We all rush to the ticket window. That's singular. Khartoum is a city of over a million, bigger than Boston, but the airport has only one ticket window. At 5:58, I make it to the counter. They tell me I'll have to wait. Maybe an hour, they say. Maybe five.

It brings to mind three letters Westerners often use here. A-W-A. Africa Wins Again.

If you know Africa, you can live here pretty well. All you have to do is drop your Western expectations. For most, that takes six months, but once you get there, you're there. I was having dinner with a U. S. Embassy official in Khartoum. As he was telling me about crop production, the lights suddenly went out. The whole place went pitch. I sat up in shock. The official kept talking, didn't even miss a comma.

"What's going on?" I said.

For the first time, he seemed to notice.

"Oh that," he said. "Happens all the time. Last August, we lost power just about the whole month. Anyway, so the whole key is sorghum. . .."

At the end of dinner, I asked him for his home phone number. He started to laugh.

"Home phone?" he said. "I've only been here a few years."

He was not joking. It can take years - that's years - to get a phone installed in Africa, even if you're a government official. Once you do, you find they're often nothing more than an ornament.

I spent almost three hours one afternoon trying to make a single call. It was not a rinky-dink line, either. I was calling the U. S. Embassy. From the Khartoum Hilton. I must have dialed more than 50 times. Finally, I got through. Ten seconds later, the connection slipped away. You can go through a lot of aspirin in Africa.

After a few days in the Sudan, I began to notice there is a single favorite subject among Americans. Beer. Even the women talk beer. It's not just that the whole country is legally dry. The place is also parched. You feel as if your mouth is constantly lined with dust, chiefly because it is. One relief worker told me all she dreams about is frosted glasses. Personally, I've always hated beer. After three days in the Sudan, I would have paid $50 for a six-pack.

It is now 7 a.m. Finally, they let me sign in. I head for the waiting lounge, where I spot a guy in a pilot's uniform. He tells me he's a member of the Nairobi flying crew. At last, someone with information. I ask him when the plane is due. He shrugs.

"Your guess is as good as mine," he says.

I ask him where the plane is. He lights a cigarette.

"Lost, I think," he says. Then he leans back and pulls his flight cap over his eyes. He seems used to this.

It is an attitude I'm trying to learn.

It takes a restaurant cashier 15 minutes to ring up your bill. It takes an hour to change American dollars into local money. Government officials often go home for the day at 2 p.m. And if you do find them at work, it's no victory. In Ethiopia, I had to kill two hard hours in the Ministry of Censorship getting approval to take my film out of the country. It wasn't that there was a lot to do, it's just that

no one was in a huge hurry to do it. Maybe tomorrow, people say. Maybe next week.

Still, there is something here that makes up for all of it. The people are the most engaging I've met anywhere. I guess that sounds a bit cliche, even patronizing, but I don't mean it that way. The truth is, I've only gotten one cold reception in Africa, and that was from a U.N. official who grew up in New Jersey.

There is also the payoff of discovery. Even if you've just wasted five hours waiting in bureaucracies for permission papers - with no success - the sight of a camel walking through a downtown street will make the day worth it.

Sometimes, the mesh between East and West is startling. One night in Khartoum, I walked into the Hilton's downstairs lounge. I saw a swarthy black Moslem in wrapped headress and white robe. He was bent forward in great concentration. I thought he was praying to the east. Then I looked close. He was playing Space Invaders. He had an excellent score.

I look at my watch. It is 8:30 a.m., the plane now five hours late. I have spent most of the time sitting with a Parisian. Like me, he is booked on the Nairobi flight. Unlike me, he was due to catch a connection home, in Nairobi, at 8:15 a.m. So much for his connection. There probably won't be another Nairobi-Paris flight for days. I tell him I'm sorry. He does the only thing you can do if you want to survive in Africa. He shrugs. And he smiles. And then, in a heavy French accent, he speaks one word:

"Inshallah."

I smile back and, in English, tell him Africa wins again. ■

" It can take years - that's years - to get a phone installed in Africa, even if you're a government official. Once you do, you find they're often nothing more than an ornament".

Friday, December 21, 1984

NAIROBI, Kenya - I'd heard about Mathare in the States, Nairobi's astonishing slum, reaching through more than a mile of urban valley. Because drought and population have damaged Kenya's north country, lately, slowly, Mathare has begun to take on a new cast, as has much poverty in the lands I'd come to visit.

Most of my work here has been in the countryside - it is the obvious place drought touches, but drought has echoes. Drought breaks the people of the country, leaving them only the city as refuge. Mathare is part of drought.

I arrive here in early afternoon. As soon as I begin to walk its center path, I am reminded of a line from a movie. All Westerners become as children when they first see the great ghettos of the Third World. I can only stare.

"It has been said that Mathare is not the Third World, it is the Fourth World".

A social worker named Ibrahim Oduoris is my escort.

"Yes," he says, "more from the country all the time."

There is everywhere the smell of refuse. The footpaths, even deep down, are at times more refuse than dirt. I see an old man stooped over a puddle of the filthiest of water, using it to wash. When you stand in the center of Mathare, there does not seem to be a way out.

More than 120,000 people live here. It is of a density hard to imagine. It is not vertical density, like the ghettos of America. Our housing projects would be an unimagined luxury here.

In Mathare the roofs rise only six feet off the ground. There are fires here often, and no electricty.

It is strange to see mud huts in the heart of a modern city. Worse than mud huts, really. These are huts made of the refuse of a city, discarded wood and tin. Stone and bone and trash. Shacks against shacks, built on dirt stomped to hardness, though always turned back to mud when it rains. It has been said that Mathare is not the Third World, it is the Fourth World.

It would not be correct to say this place is here because of drought. It was here long before drought. But it is beginning now, this new sociology of flight from the land. More and more, Mathare will be where drought ends.

We go into the darkness of a woman's house. Her name is Priscilla Wangiru. She lives with six children in this one room. I expect to be received with suspicion. There is only warmth. Mathare may breed some anger, but it also breeds an aching trust that any outsider could be an answer.

Does she like it here?

Of course not.

Where would she like to go?

Anyplace else.

She sits for a picture. I'll remember for some time the earnestness of her pose. She seemed to believe, really believe, that perhaps this photograph could change things.

And then there is Omdurman.

Omdurman, in the Sudan - Khartoum's parallel city, wrapped just across the Nile.

But that is not the Omdurman I speak of. I speak of the city outside the city. The new city, spawned in the desert only recently. Unlike Mathare, Omdurman is drought's purest creation. It is 23,000 people all driven here by the wasting of the land.

I went there with a relief worker named Salim. We drove out of Khartoum, moving from asphalt streets to streets of sand, from cars to camels, then suddenly, into a crowded plain - Khartoum's vast Bedouin market, full of goats and produce and ornaments. Hollywood's Arabia.

There were no roads. We just made our way, our doors skimming craftsmans' stands. For 20 minutes, we were lost in it. And then we emerged into a gap of nothing.

And finally, in the distance, Omdurman.

The new Omdurman. I expected density. It was somehow unsettling to see that it wasn't that way. It is a vast plain dotted with 5,000 tiny shelters stretching to the heat waves of the horizon. From above, it would look like scattered tumbleweeds. There is silence except for the wind.

It is the demography of this continent. Too many people over-using the fragile land, overgrazing it, taking too many trees for firewood, the weather finally finishing the land off, leaving the people in a place with nothing, until they flee to the city, where there is also nothing.

I should not use the word shelter for the dwelling places of Omdurman. Each is four sticks with cloth draped over the top, the sides open to the desert - shower stalls with sand floors. Between four and seven people live inside.

I am beginning to think I have visited too many desperation camps. But it has given me the tool of comparison. Each seems to have its own mood. Here, it is the mood of the breaking of spirit. You can feel it. It's like the feeling of cold.

I heard about Omdurman from an American development worker named Jim Geenen. He told me what I would see here, and then he told me what I would not see. I would not see the psychological, he said. I would not see what happens underneath when the families of a noble tribe are turned to begging.

"This man used to own the stars," said Geenen. "Had goats, cattle, sheep, the whole prairie. Now he's got a few starving kids and a couple of sticks for a house. What would that do to you?"

It is a life of nothingness, each day offering only two things - the heat of the desert and the wait for government food. The people here are only existing.

I find myself thinking that if there is ever a final war, this is how the survivors will live.

With Salim, I move on, trying to find how far Omdurman stretches.

He stops to speak with one of the families. He comes back in the car and is silent for a long time. I ask what it is.

"I asked what tribe he was from," he says. "It used to be one of the wealthiest tribes in the Sudan."

We stop at another dwelling place, and then another, and another still.

How long were you a farmer?

Ten years, 20, 40. No, I've never seen it this bad. Never seen camels die.

And now?

I wait, I wait for rain. And no, there has not been good rain for four years.

For 10 minutes, we continue driving, still unable to find the end of Omdurman. But something has changed. We are now in the outer reaches, the place of the new arrivals, those distant from the distribution of food. They eye our car differently from the others. We stop to see.

One comes toward us. He runs like a frightened man, but at us, not away. Then five come, then 20, then more, all running. They come against the car, surrounding the car, hands coming through the window.

"Very bad," says Salim, "very bad." He tries to go forward, but they are at the fenders now. They will not move. They press until 10 arms are inside. One reaches for my camera.

Finally, Salim guns the engine, and guns it again, and keeps doing it until we are able to creep through, then break away.

We drive back through Omdurman. He tells me he has never seen Sudanese people beg before. He tells me it is against their tradition.

He tells me he would like to go home. ■

I had never seen so dense a ghetto. It's called Mathare. It's in Nairobi. For many, it is where drought ends.

Sunday, December 23, 1984

NYERI, Kenya - I have come to safari country to let things settle in. This trip was to witness, but you can witness too much. Those with experience in seeing this side of Africa warned me that afterward, there would be bad days, and I should make time for them.

So I am making time. And I find an odd reaction. I find, after two weeks of refugees and famine camps, that I'm feeling uplifted.

I don't mean to diminish the pain I've seen. But there is a thread I've been following that's left a deeper impression than the victims.

The healers.

Perhaps you have to seek out the worst of suffering to find the best of souls. Since coming to Africa, I've found a few.

I was sitting near the Korem feeding camp in Ethiopia one night, feeling sorry for myself. The back country can be hard on the Western spirit. It's not just what you see, it's the way you live. Bad water, bad road, no comfort.

I was having dinner with a woman who'd just finished five years in the Peace Corps - Nanette from Cleveland. She did her two, then kept reenlisting.

Gabon, she said. I asked what Gabon is like.

Hot, she said. Furnace heat. No movies, no TV, no newspapers. You get sick, too. Dysentery. Malaria. The usual stuff. No running water, either. Or electricity. The food tends to be bizarre. Like camel's hump. Or even cat.

Then, of course, there are the long work days. And the lonely nights.

"Sounds pretty grim," I said.

"I loved it," she said.

She was not a masochist. Or on a religious trip. There is just something about the Third World, she said. She could not get more specific, except to say it's not simply that there's a need, it's what it gives you back.

Who are these Westerners? What kind of person would so willingly trade comfort for jobs in places the rest of us hope we never even have to look at?

They seemed to be everywhere. Several times a day, I'd see Western faces in a hotel lobby and ask what brought them here. Red Cross, said one. From Canada, said another, we're doing a water project down south. I'm a doctor, said an American from Idaho. No special reason, just thought I owed this.

Most began with the Peace Corps, or a private group like it, figuring a year or two would be enough, then time to come home. And they did come home, but they couldn't shake it. Living in the West left them with a restlessness.

The restlessness grew until, eventually, they felt they had to go back. So they did, signing on with something like Save the Children or UNICEF. And after that tour they did another, soon finding the Third World a career.

When I was in Korem, I met a thirtyish Frenchman who looked like a Beach Boy. He was appropriately named Jean Luis Blond. Had he chosen surfing in California, he'd have had his pick. Instead, he'd come to do a year as a famine camp medical aide. He said the accommodations in Korem were almost too luxurious. I laughed. He was living in a cell. He didn't laugh.

"I especially like the desert," he said. "There are no police to help you, no hospitals. You're totally responsible for yourself."

"Why do you like that?" I asked.

"It is better way to be a man," he said.

He didn't mean it macho. Sometimes, broken English is more honest than careful English.

I asked him about showers and movies and steaks. The good life.

"When you have too much comfort," he said, "you can't get a good human experience. You forget what's important."

For example?

"When you are 500 kilometers from the nearest town," he said, "you know exactly what is a glass of water."

They are of different countries, different personalities, but they share a common gene, a thread.

One morning, five of us left Korem by truck, hoping to find a plane to Addis Ababa. Two doctors were with me, hoping to make an important afternoon meeting. I was in no hurry, but began pacing nevertheless, looking from the sky to my watch. The doctors sat patiently. I think they were amused by me.

Finally, I asked if they thought there was any hope.

"If it comes it comes," said one. "And if it doesn't. . ." He shrugged and said there is no gain in anxiety. He learned that from Africa. It is something they don't teach in the West.

There are other threads. Nobody, for example, seemed to swagger. Maybe Africa teaches that, too - that there's no room to be self-impressed.

One night I was staying in a relief worker's house when a rather sweaty, dirt-streaked young man walked in. His name was Rob Frey, from America. I asked what he'd been up to.

"Spent the day setting up tents," he said.

"You specialize in shelter?" I asked.

"No," he said. "I'm a doctor. But they needed some help."

I waited for him to do some griping. Instead, he said it felt good to work up a callous or two for a change.

I knew something was missing when I first came to the African backland, but it took me a few weeks to realize what. It was whining.

They don't whine about being late for the hairdresser. Or having to sleep on a dirt floor. Or treating 200 critical patients laid out in the most unsanitary of makeshift sheds. They don't whine if they get a cold, or malaria. What happens, happens. You just deal with it.

I'd like to tell you now about Michael Pelly.

He was a 30-year-old doctor from England. He'd been doing Africa for six years and was back for six months more of famine medicine in Ethiopia.

We were talking in Korem, at night.

I told him I found it surprising to find so many doctors here.

"You'd have it so easy back home," I said.

"Perhaps that's why I left," he said.

We'd finished dinner at the relief worker's compound and were now walking down the town's dirt road. It was very dark out. Our room was a mile away. Of course, there were no cabs. No vehicles, period. Dogs barked, goats wandered by.

We walked for a while in quiet. He was the first to break it.

"My brother thinks I must be mad," he said. He seemed to enjoy the thought.

I took the opening.

"So why not settle down?

"Maybe someday," he said. "But you don't want to do it too early."

I asked why he does this.

"I haven't really thought about it," he said.

"I know why I write," I said. "You must have a why, too."

He gave a curious answer. He said that in some ways, he found it more civilized than England.

I asked how that was possible.

The street by now was pitch dark. Black Africans kept walking in and out of the shadows. We were the only whites.

"This," he said. "This right now. I've been mugged in London. I've never been mugged in Africa."

We made it back to our rooms. It was almost midnight. We stood in the dirt hallway, washing our hands and faces in an old basin filled with cold water. We took turns training flashlights on each other.

"She was not a masochist. There is just something about the Third World, she said. She could not get more specific, except to say it's not simply that there's a need, it's what it gives you back".

I could feel the mud beneath my feet. We paused to spray our beds with insecticide. The temperature was about 40. As we waited for the fumes to clear, I had visions of a hot fireplace, a late movie and maybe some carry-out Chinese food.

I asked Pelly if he ever daydreamed about luxuries.

"Quite a bit," he said.

I waited for him to tell me about penthouse suites or ocean beaches.

"What I'd really like," he said, "would be to get into Addis for a good wash-up. Just for an hour or two."

The Peace Corps worker from Gabon talked about choices. She told me the Africans she was working with found her particularly puzzling. How could you come here, they kept asking. How could you leave America for dirt floors and no electricity?

I asked how she answered it.

"Pretty simple," she said. "Africa helps you see what's important and what isn't."

I suppose, in the end, it's the answer we're all after. ■

Monday, December 24, 1984

NYERI, Kenya - I have been in Kenya two days now, and it's taken me that long to realize what's so different about the sky. There are clouds here. It is the first time I've seen clouds since coming to Africa.

I had begun to wonder what happened to the myth of this continent. I traveled here expecting deep forest and wide river. I found only sand.

I suppose where I am now is Africa as it once was, before weather and population began to turn it. Maybe that's why I came to this lodge amid the wildlife, so I'd have one good piece to keep. Here, mountains are full of green, and the fields are, too, and last night, under a high moon, I saw a white rhino coming slowly out of the woods.

"Road tends to change you. It breaks you loose from routine, giving you a new passion for things different, but also a loneliness that makes you just want to come back to what you know."

It's showed me something I had not been sure about: Yes, there is much pain in Africa, but there's much beauty too.

Because it takes some doing to send these stories across an ocean, the things I write are printed a few days after they're done. I'm now realizing this one should appear the day before Christmas. A good time to pause, especially from where I sit. This is the first day I've had on this trip to think about something other than drought and hunger.

I find myself looking back and forward at the same time. Stopping on a journey will get you to doing that. I'm not the most well-traveled of people. For me, these past few weeks have been a lot of road.

Road tends to change you. It breaks you loose from routine, giving you a new passion for things different, but also a loneliness that makes you just want to come back to what you know.

I'm not sure if taking a trip like this alone is the best way to do it, but it's probably the most telling. You learn what you have and what you don't have.

Road leaves you with no choice but to reach into your center to get through whatever you've come against. Airport porters and hotel doormen will carry your bags, but that's the least of your weight. The harder weight, the weight that's with you on bad nights and first hours in new countries, that weight's all on you. It tests your resilience, strengthening it in the end, I suppose, but stretching it awfully thin while you're out there. This is not the kind of trip you'd want to take if you were going through a bad time.

Still, even then, you'd probably come away seeing that it's not as hard to swim as you thought. You can't know that until you come against things. I remember being told something similar by a whitewater raft guide.

The test, he said, isn't whether you've navigated a smooth, uneventful trip. The test is how you do when you get in trouble, when you snag a current and find yourself drawn suddenly and swiftly toward rock.

I've learned a few things from Africa. It's taught me a pretty good lesson about getting beyond defeats. You can miss it in America because things work so well there.

Here they don't. Planes don't fly, people don't show up, soldiers make you turn back. Here you get defeats, sometimes big ones, every day. I used to think you reacted to such things by throwing your shoulder against the door a few times, and if it still didn't give, then you pounded sand.

When I first came here, I saw people reacting a different way. Westerners in Africa have learned to shrug off defeats. It's the way things are, they say. Inshallah.

But that's not really it. I was only looking at the surface. In truth, what they do is first shrug it off, and then, right away, push for something else. Something different. Never at the same door - that's the key. You can usually tell when it's not going to open. They find another.

Africa teaches that you have no choice.

It may be true that you just ran out of medicine, and the nearest supply is two days by truck. It is still no excuse to write off a patient. That's not a possibility. Your only choice is to calmly sit down and come up with a new treatment. You just do it, even if it means cutting new ground. A sick infant and no incubator? All right, make an incubator. Figure a way. A different way.

I still spend my share of time dwelling on frustration, but slowly, I've begun to pick that up. I'd spent weeks back in the States setting up a flight to a certain area of Sudan. The day I got there, it fell through. It put my whole plan for that country right under. I spent two hours back on the phone that day, trying to make it happen. A waste of time. Then, distraught, I called a few numbers to find out what else was going on. A door I hadn't even thought about opened up. It turned out to be a better story.

In the end, defeat's not that hard. You just offset it with a different kind of victory. The only rule is to keep moving. If I can carry that back home, it won't be a bad diploma.

The road's also taught me something about work. It can prove more of a lifeline than I'd realized.

The Westerners I've met have all been living in the worst of conditions, and all have explained it the same way. You can get past most things if you see your work as sustenance.

It both takes your strength, they said, and gives it back. It is the sapper of resilience and the source of it. You work until you are exhausted, and then you stop, until the stopping begins to exhaust you more, pushing you back to it as a refuge, a friend, a reason.

They aren't workaholics - people who see work as an escape. Those I've met here see it as something inner. Yes, they need the pay-

check, but they need the psychic salary more. I've yet to meet a Westerner in Africa who watches the clock. And this would have been a much harder trip if I'd have had less to write.

There's one final diploma to talk about. I guess I should admit that another reason I came to safari country was a personal one. Hemingway happens to be one of my favorite writers. I wanted to see the part of the world he drew so much from.

One of his most famous stories is about this place - "The Snows of Kilimanjaro" - and I thought this would be a good time to reread it. And I did. But I had some trouble with it.

The story's about regret mostly, about a dying writer looking back at all the things he'd left undone and unwritten, all the unrealized plans. It did not fit with what I'd been thinking about since coming here.

The side of Africa I've seen has not been about the missing of things, it's about the pursuit of them. About not giving up. Everyone I've met working to solve this crisis is a believer in what can be.

I paused in safari country to think. As I wrote this piece, a baboon climbed to the deck behind me. I left my chair to capture the moment.

It's the seed you pick up here, an understanding that what it's about is taking things on. You don't ask whether it's possible but whether it's worthy enough to try. And however it falls, there is no reason to sit down and chronicle things unrealized, because the getting there is in the trying.

I awoke at dawn. Africa has colors like no other place. The sky was smoke and rose. I could see snow on the top of Mt. Kenya. The bush buck and water buffalo were still at the pond.

So much beauty, so much pain. I was beginning to understand Africa's draw. There is something about that combination.

Soon, I will fly west to see the desert. ■■■

Tuesday, December 25, 1984

DORI, Burkina Faso - Finally, I am about to see true desert. It is the symbol of this journey: the final wasting of the land.

I have chosen Dori carefully. It is said that slowly, desert is claiming North Africa. Every year, it moves south another three miles, another five, in some places 10. On the crest of that movement, the story of food crisis is told. Dori is on the crest.

It sits 150 miles north of the capital. There is no good road, just a four-wheel-drive path. My plane leaves at 10 a.m. I am traveling with Baba Philipe of Save the Children. For years, they have been in Dori making a stand against the weather. Lately, the weather has been overwhelming them. We are bringing up our own food and water - there is little left where we are going.

Our carrier is Air Burkina, the national airline. Its fleet consists of two planes. Actually, three, but one has been broken since January. We are lucky, we leave only two hours late.

I see it happen from the air. Mile by mile. The green fades. Soon, though, I lose view of the land. There is a heavy fog outside, only it is not fog. This is the season of the harmatan, a strange steady wind that carries Sahara dust hundreds, even thousands, of miles, filling all the air of West Africa. Many who live here wear rags over their mouths for months. I cannot even see the sun.

It makes plane travel difficult. We fly over Dori's dirt strip once, but we lose it in the harmatan when we turn for the approach.

We try again, and miss again.

It takes us five tries to get it right, and even then we only find the strip in its middle, lurching down violently with barely enough runway to stop.

We climb down to the sand of Dori. Philipe says never again, from now on, he'll travel by jeep - this was too close. Another Save the Children worker smiles and tells him to look on the bright side. In Burkina Faso, there's little chance of a mid-air collision.

Because I have just come from Kenya's good country, the starkness here hits me with a clarity. The town is a black-and-white photograph. No, in a way it is worse. There is only one shade here. The walls are sand and the streets are sand. The sky is the color of sand. Even the trees are covered with the fine film of the Sahara.

I ask Philipe why he would want to work in such a place. He answers that he himself has wondered why the people of Dori stay here. But they do, and that is the answer. You see souls who hold to hope in a hopeless place, and it makes you want to hope with them.

Until a few weeks ago, I'd never heard of this country. It used to be Upper Volta, then came a coup and a name change, and now the drought has brought it an odd kind of prominence. Go to Burkina, people in the hunger business told me, you will see how it is happening.

It is how I've come to be in one of the most obscure towns in one of the most obscure of nations. As I walk among the sand-walled huts, I at first feel as though I've left the planet. In fact, here in Dori, I have perhaps come closer to it than I have ever been before.

America, in the end, is not the world. In numbers, the true world is the Third World. And this is how it lives: not in cities, but in villages poised on the edge of conditions, people trying simply to wring bread from hard sand.

We stop in Save the Children's stark Dori compound. "This is where Jerry stays," says Philipe.

He is speaking of Jerry Pasela, the group's Burkina director. He is an American from Cleveland. He lives in the capital, but spends half his time - two weeks a month - working here in the desert, a day's jeep ride from his family. He has been in Dori almost five years.

In these past weeks, I have begun to grow hardened to the suffering of Africa. But there is something I've seen that still continues to surprise me: Walking into places of utter desolation and finding an American there by choice.

Philipe tells me even he is confused by it. For his own commitment, there is a reason - it is his country and these his people. But his boss, he says, is different. Why, Philipe asks, would an American come across an ocean for this?

I wonder who this Jerry Pasela is. I decide I must visit him when I get back to the capital. Philipe and I drive into the desert. I had not realized it before, but there are two deserts in North Africa. There is the great Sahara, where almost nothing can survive. And then, just beneath it, there is the Sahel. The Sahel is the crest of hunger. I am in the heart of it now.

The land is harsher than I thought. There is as much stone and rock as sand. It reminds me of some of the sun-killed mountains of Ethiopia.

And for the first time, I realize how big this drought is. It is as big as all of America, and even bigger. I have now traveled 3,000 miles and I have yet to outrun it.

It is almost as if it has been mapped out for me, east to west, in neatly packaged stages. I have gone from famine camp to refugee camp to land turned to desert. Slowly, level by level, I am moving backward through the progression of starvation. First Ethiopia, then Ethiopia six months ago, now Ethiopia a year ago.

Philipe tells me how it has happened. April came and they sowed crop, waiting for the rains to lift it. But there was no rain, and the seeds burned.

So they sowed again in July, and again, the seeds burned.

A third time they tried, and a third time it happened. Finally, rains did come, but by then they were out of seed. Nor were the rains good rains. They came harsh and quick, cutting and depleting a hardened soil.

The statistical men now measure the loss of crop at 90 percent.

The old men say the last time the weather conspired this destructively was 1926 - and that was a green time. The livestock men point to the hides of their animals and say it is beginning, soon the herds will start to die.

There are two other signs. From the countryside, hungry Bedouins are moving into Dori - newcomers.

And in town, there is the Save the Children health center. A program has begun for malnourished infants. The capacity is 30. The program is full. And the outpatient load is building.

I sleep this night in a lightless room beneath a mosquito net. Before I drift off, I hear laughter and drums. Not jungle drums, but the kind you might hear in an American city - the sound of rhythm and youth. Every night, the teenagers of Dori gather to dance in the dust, to flirt and hope for connection. As I lie here, I think of teenagers back home, doing the same, being young in the towns they grew up in. Certain things seem to be universal.

I wonder if these children may soon find themselves in a feeding camp.

There is no plane scheduled back to the capital for four days, so we decide to do the trip by vehicle. The harmatan is bad throughout. The dirt road is worse - half the time, it is impassable, forcing us to wind through the desert.

We pass too many goats, which are killing the land, and too much cut wood, which is also killing the land.

The drive takes seven hours. My back is shot. It will not be easy to truck food up to Dori.

That evening, I find Jerry Pasela in his office. He tells me he heard about my plane landing; he says it is why he never flies Burkina anymore.

"Those kind of landings get old real fast," he says.

He has a deep voice, big forearms, and is unique among Westerners I've met here. He is 44. It makes him the old man of relief work. It is as rare to find that age in the bush of Africa as in the fields of American sport.

I get right to it, asking how he copes with it. He is not in the world's garden spot.

"Hardly," he says. "And it's getting worse."

I use the word famine. He is matter-of-fact.

"Definitely," he says. "It's coming."

I ask him about his projects, and he goes for a half-hour nonstop.

He takes out an elaborate project chart: gardens, irrigation, reforestation. I glance around the office. There are charts everywhere - it looks a bit like a war room. I think, if given a choice between this battle and a military one, I would risk facing weaponry. Pasela's enemy seems more difficult.

He admits it. He says the scientist in him has no faith in Dori's land.

This, too, is where drought ends. The tents of hunger's refugees are throughout Africa.

"So why are you there?" I ask.

He tells me about the other part of him. He tells me how he was once a teacher. And how a certain kind of moment made teaching worth it - those few times a student's face engaged.

"Something turned inside that human being," he said, "and at that moment, they grew. And would keep growing."

He sees the same look here.

"Suddenly," he says, "people we're working with will realize their own creativity, and it'll change their lives."

Still, I say, the land is dying.

He agrees. But that's all right. Even if you can't win, you can hold things back, and there is victory in that. He says it is all right to fail, but not to give up. I leave him, hoping that someday, if I am lucky, I will learn to have half as much faith as he.

The elders of a village near Dori. They gave me a chair, took a mat for themselves, and for an hour, they told me about hunger.

Before I left Dori, I asked to see one of the outlying villages.

Philipe took me there. My arrival was announced. A decision was made. A journalist was here. It was important enough for a meeting with the elders.

Twenty of them came, and 20 others stood nearby - 40 black African villagers, one white American. Children peeked from around trees.

The elders brought me a chair and laid out a mat for themselves in front of me. We had to triple-translate. They spoke in tribal tongue. A villager put it into French and Philipe put the French into English.

I told them I'd come from America, where crops are always bountiful, to find out how they're able to live in the desert. They all laughed. The contrast, they explained.

I asked if they'd ever talked to an Ameri-

can journalist. No, they said, but John Denver. He was here on a hunger tour the month before. They asked if that was a good as a journalist. I told them it was close.

The harmatan seemed to pick up. I wore chinos, an L.L. Bean shirt and Rockport shoes. They wore robes.

They asked why I came.

I told them that food problems in villages like this are now a great issue in America.

They said they have always seen Americans as human kin, they were glad we saw them as the same.

I asked how bad hunger had become here.

They laughed again. Look at us, they said. What do you think?

I asked about the harvest.

They've never seen a year this bad.

Is there back-up food in storage?

Yes. But it will last only a month. Then, no one knows.

They listened intently. They laughed often. In America, poverty seems to dim the spirit. Here, there was no sign of that.

What would have happened without Save the Children's food programs?

They laughed again. They would have all had to leave by now.

And where will you go if you do have to leave?

Now there was no laughter. This was a difficult issue. This, they do not know.

We talked for an hour. They asked if I had any final thoughts. I could only say I was sorry for what had happened to their land.

They each took my hand, and thanked me, asking if I would tell my countrymen that they need our help and embrace it with gratitude.

Then they said they had something to show me. The walk took 10 minutes.

We came upon a stand of trees. What lay on the other side made me stop. It was a vegetable garden covering more than an acre, as lush as any in America. It was the first color I'd seen in Dori.

There are five wells here, and all day, dozens of villagers work them, drawing water, asking all the wells have to give.

This should not be able to work. This soil is not even as good as beach sand. I do not know how much longer they can maintain. But right now, this one corner is holding.

If there is a single image I would hope to carry home with me from Africa, it is that garden. I now understand why an American from Cleveland has given five years of his life to this piece of the desert. It is something to think about on this Christmas Day.

Life is being made to happen in this most inhuman of places, and it says much about believing in the not-quite-possible. ■■■

FADA N'GOURMA, Burkina Faso - Steinbeck once wrote about men like these. Men of nature and men of science. Men who bring life from seed in places where life was not meant to spring. "These are great men," he wrote.

I am reminded of this now as I stand in a farmer's field in a desert village in the countryside of Burkina Faso.

The soil on these five acres is dust and sand. The weather this year was catastrophic. But somehow, the crop that emerged was of Iowa caliber. Great men have been here.

I'd heard about this patch of earth before I left America, I'd now traveled 11,000 miles to see it. It seems almost a humorous errand. My fantasy of foreign correspondence wasn't exactly to come poking around an old shed, staring at bags of grain in a country most people have never heard of. Still, it may be one of the most important moments of this journey.

We have all been writing about hunger, but it's not the answer, of course. Neither is there solution in the charity of nations. There is only one answer, one test that must be passed - finding a way to coax crop from desert.

Right now, I am seeing its success. I am seeing one man's patch of bounty in the midst of a failed harvest. And I am thinking: If it can be done here, it can be done.

Whose work is this?

I was told his name was Graham Owen. He is the agricultural director of Partnership for Productivity, another one of those American groups that finds its calling in a place most Americans will never care about.

I expected an elder statesman of the science of soil. Owen turned out to be a 29-year-old Peace Corps veteran who looked like one of those guys who never studied in college because the snack bar was more compelling.

He works in obscurity. His manner is easy. If there are heroes of this issue, he is one.

You have to see this land to understand how hard it is to coax crop off it, and how deep the faith of those who try. It's not just a farmer's nightmare, it's an aesthetic's too.

And Graham Owen loves this land. It's why he spent months working with the farmer who owns it. And why, now, he seeks only one thing - more bad soil with which to do the same.

There are people like him all over Africa, lovers of hopeless land. They spend their hours in dusty offices and dry fields, lost in the mysteries of seed and soil.

They have an odd twist to their personalities. They feel there are few things duller in this world than good, rich earth. It is too easy. They turn instead to places where green life is almost impossible. They have a need to make things grow where things should not be able to.

They even love desert. They love the thought of beating it.

I met such a man in Khartoum. His name was Eric Witt. He is our agricultural development officer in the Sudan. Most people carry with them photos of their children. He carries photos of sorghum plants.

"You have to see this land to understand how hard it is to coax crop off it, and how deep the faith of those who try".

We were having dinner in the Khartoum Hilton. He told me that compared with the Sudan, Phoenix, Ariz., is a rain forest. He also said that Africa is the world's only continent that has seen food production decline steadily.

Both thoughts exhilarated him. It is the nature of this kind of person. They welcome climatic disaster. It gives them something to conquer.

He seemed like the type who carried a slide rule in high school. His office had strange decor - the walls were lined with a dozen samples of harvested sorghum. He picked up the most fruitful strain and shook it at me.

"Is this stuff beautiful," he said, "or what?"

I asked why this was so important.

He was incredulous.

"Why?" he said. "I'll tell you why."

He began scrawling figures over scrap paper. Then he looked at me in triumph. This year, he said, this strain gave four times the yield of other strains. And it did it in drought country - sorghum swelling defiantly beneath a killing sun. A 400 percent increase, he repeated. It is the statistic of a continent's survival.

I asked how it was done. Witt spent 10 minutes telling me of a scientist who worked six years with 3,000 varieties of seed, crossing and crossing them again until he'd created a new and great seed equipped to prevail against the weather.

The scientist who did this will mean nothing to most people, but his name is worth mentioning here for history. Let it be known that in coming years, many Africans will not suffer as much as they might have, and many others will not die, because a man named Gebisa Ejeta, the mad scientist of sorghum, spent some time in his laboratory.

Men of nature. Men of science. It brings us back to Graham Owen. He came to Burkina Faso to make the soil work, coming with degrees from America, but knowing, as do all those who understand the Third World, that here, American knowledge is not good enough. Or perhaps too good. You cannot master bankrupt soil with knowledge from a nation where soil is rich. Here, he had to learn and unlearn at the same time, immersing himself in desert, and in the places of this nation that research it.

He came to know desert seed and desert fertilizer. He came to know, as intimately as a sailor knows tide, how this land shifts with the weather. And gradually, he pieced together a tissue of approach. There would be simple dirt dikes to control erosion, weather breaks to block the harmatan wind. There would be just the right seed, just the right fertilizer and just enough plowing, but not too much. And new tree lines, new hedges, too, all to chip back at the desert's press.

There would be no magic here, no master stroke, just a range of adjustments with one great goal - to keep just enough moisture in this moistureless place, not only for this year, but next year, too, and next decade. If it is all to last, the soil must be replenished even as you draw from it. You must repay it for what you take.

And Owen understood that there must be one other thing. It is not enough to be a man of the laboratory. It will mean nothing if your theories impress only the world's great authorities. The world's authorities mean nothing here.

There is only one level of approval you must seek, and it is from the poorest, most powerless person in Africa, the farmer.

Owen's organization saw this. They anchored themselves in this village called Fada, offering not just knowledge, but loans to make it possible for farmers to use the knowledge.

A structure of commerce grew. And the interest of one particular farmer was such that he adopted all the techniques in a focal experiment.

The farmer's name is Moyenga Soyuba. He is a good spirited but unimpressive man who, like many, has been on the edge of poverty most of his life. With Owen's help, he used

"He came to know desert seed and desert fertilizer. He came to know, as intimately as a sailor knows tide, how this land shifts with the weather."

the techniques. The seed and the dikes and the plowing. And together, they waited.

His main crop this year was millet, a kind of wheat. His neighbors all grew the same. With the coming of drought, their harvests failed. His grew seven feet high. Instead of harvesting the eight sacks he usually drew in the past, he harvested 22. In this year of no rain, he gathered the yield of his life.

Had someone told me all this two months ago, I might have cared only a little. But I have been in Africa too long to not care. I have seen enough barren ground and famine camps to know the meaning of this grain-filled shed.

There are only 22 sacks in there, but they hold more promise than the great buildings of the continent's great cities.

If Graham Owen were to read this article, he might think it overdone. He does not see himself as the creator of a great plan. He will tell you he only wants to help farmers. And that is why there is so much hope in what he does.

When I began this journey, I had lunch in Rome with Millicent Fenwick, our ambassador to the Food and Agricultural Organization. She spoke of how she and her colleagues, ambassadors from all the world, spend their days debating food policy in FAO's general assembly room.

"But none of that will mean a thing," she said, "if you don't get down in the village and work with the people struggling to produce. Who is the small farmer? What does he want?"

There is the answer. In this one place, Graham Owen has found it. Ask the farmer, teach the farmer, and Africa could turn. Sow not just seed into ground, but knowledge into a mind.

In the way of a fraternity brother, Owen put his arm around his Burkina farmer friend.

"What he knows now," he said, "you can never take away from him."

I still had one doubt to share with Owen. In the end, I said, the weather will only get worse. "You can't deny that the desert's moving south," I said.

"Yes I can," he said. "I don't really accept that."

I suppose that is how all hard battles are won - by people who won't accept losing them.

I still find it a bit odd that I came so far to see a few sacks of millet. There are more momentous issues for a journalist to cover. There are wars and diplomacy and great politics.

But right now, as I stand here in this dusty field, none of that seems as important as this shed.

Great men have been here. ■■■■

Graham Owen with his friend and client, Moyenga Soyuba. Together, in the midst of drought, they made a corner of the desert bloom.

Friday, December 28, 1984

TIMBUKTU - I am close to this journey's end. As I enter its last few days, I've decided to go to Timbuktu. For 600 years, its name has been a symbol of Africa's bounty. Now, there is starvation even here.

It sits in the north country of Mali, on the lip of the Sahara. The capital of Mali is Bamako. The day I arrive there, I am told no one has been able to get to Timbuktu for 12 days. It is two hours by plane, and we are in the season of the sandstorm.

There is no weather like this in the world. When the harmatan winds begin, the desert rises like a cloud, blocking all vision.

Now, the airline has scheduled a special flight before dawn, hoping the night's cool will settle enough sand to help us see the runway. I get to the airport at 4 a.m. Soon after, we lift into the air. A woman on the plane tells me this is her fourth try. On each of the first three, they had to turn back halfway.

There are two great forces below me - the desert and the Niger River. We follow the Niger, until we lose it in the harmatan's haze, and now I lean back, feeling a deep fatigue. It is not so much the pace of these last few weeks, it is something else.

It is possible to cross more of North Africa than I have, but not much more. I am almost 4,000 miles from Ethiopia, where I began, and I have found only an unbroken band of pain, and I am very tired.

This day, nature turns its favor upon us. The runway is visible. The plane touches down.

Again, as has happened so often in this continent, I find a Westerner here who has embraced a mission in a corner of nowhere. Her name is Marion vanDensen, a Dutchwoman who is Timbuktu's UNICEF coordinator. Her program was begun 18 months ago, when the starvation started.

You need a Land Rover to drive anywhere in Timbuktu. The roads are deep sand. The Sahara is claiming this place. There is even sand in the bread.

The city is quiet, almost desolate, but still holds a flavor of what once was. The men wear black and carry swords. The streets wind with a closed European feel, then open to an infinity of sand. Caravans of camel walk by. Once, this was Africa's hub of commerce. Now, its face is being changed by tiny, ragged tents. Newcomers.

Some might feel it is no surprise. The desert, after all, is the desert. But for those who know her, the desert can be - and has been for 1,000 years - a kind of mother. There are brief rains each season which lift grass for livestock. For centuries, millions of nomads have lived off it. Now, because of drought, it is all coming to an end.

Marion is 29. She has short blond hair. A few months ago, she says, people were eating twigs.

"And now?" I ask.

Now, she says, it is bad, but holding. There is emergency food. A slight rain came recently, lifting the lightest of grass.

Instead of famine, there is now only hunger, a lull between the starvation of last summer and the starvation that will come again soon, when the grass runs out, and the livestock again die.

At first, I have a journalist's reaction to this. I feel a disappointment at having arrived between crises. Often, we think our role is to chronicle the greatest drama. Here, I missed that.

But I'm realizing something now. Finding drama means we've come too late. In our truest role, we should warn of the approach of crises, not cover their arrival.

So now, let me tell you how it is beginning here. And let me tell you of those people of Timbuktu whom we still might save.

We drive into the desert - deep, true desert, dune blending into dune. We drive an hour, then two, the Land Rover stalling often in the sand. Vast country, harsh country. It is hard to picture anyone living out here.

But soon, we come upon a settlement.

There are 100 nomads here, and a handful of cattle. There is a feel of desperation, but both people and animals have a way about them, a pride and leanness that comes of survival on the edge.

They are growing trees. Here in the sand, in neat rows, there are hundreds of six-inch seedlings. Now, they explain, one day, there will be wood.

"How can this work?" I ask.

Marion points to a nearby well.

"Sand is fertile," she explains. "With water, you can grow."

I walk among the tents. I have seen these children before. Some have the look of photographs from feeding camps. Often, they go days without eating. Right now, it is the compassion of nations that keeps them alive.

And it makes me wonder. It is so difficult out here. I ask Marion why she is trying to help them stay.

"Because it's worse in the towns," she says.

I have moved from country to country, searching for new angles to this drought, only to keep finding the same angle.

This famine is one famine, and I am learning its riddle without answer. Nothing left in the back-country, less still in the towns, where are people to go?

The nomad chief comes over to talk. He is fluent in French. He wears a Seiko watch and smokes Marlboros.

He says they've lost most of their cattle and will probably lose the rest. He says they are beginning to settle, learn agriculture. He says they are trying to find a new way of living.

I am about to ask how long he hopes to hold out here. Then I glance at the seedlings. Trees in the Sahara. It is faith itself.

We move on, grinding through desert and dune, ridge and furrow, finally coming to a settlement called Ber.

Maybe 1,500 live here, a quarter of them newcomers. I have seen these newcomers, too. Was it Omdurman in the Sudan? Or perhaps Dori in Burkina Faso. It is all countries.

One famine.

We are met by a village elder named Mohammed. He speaks of what they all speak of first - the children. He says they have been kept alive by only one thing, food from UNICEF.

"And if it were to stop?" I ask.

"It would be a catastrophe," he says.

Four thousand miles and, still, I am having the same conversations.

But there is something different in Mali. Here, I am finding a new level.

Here, in the midst of hunger, there is still an obsession with the life of the mind. Mohammed is the settlement's most revered man for one reason - he is its school director.

I ask how there can be room for schooling in a time of famine. He explains that food is not enough. There must also be possibilities.

There is something he wants to show me. It sits in the middle of a field as parched as any I've seen. It is a solitary pipe.

"A new pump," says Marion.

"For irrigation," says Mohammed.

I look around. This is the Sahara.

"Crops?" I ask. "Here?"

If there is water, they say, there is possibility.

Slowly, Timbuktu is being overwhelmed by desert. By weather. By the changing of things. No longer is it a place of greatness.

But there is still a certain kind of greatness here. It is the greatness of Marion van-Densen, and a village elder named Mohammed.

I have already written about the severest of starvation. Today, I give you an even better drama: the faith of those who think there is still time to save a people. And who have come to try. ▮▮

The story of Mali, and of Africa, too: people of the land, moving toward help, seeing hunger's first sign - a sick child.

Sunday, December 30, 1984

TIMBUKTU, Mali - We are all of us homeless this night. They are nomads who have lost their land; I am a traveler, far from everything I am part of. Together, we are spending Christmas Eve in the desert.

We are the oddest of couplings. They wear Moslem robes; I a flannel shirt. I grew up in Chicago and live now in New England; they've known only the Sahara. I have with me enough cash to cross the ocean in a morning. If they want to visit the nearest village, 10 miles distant, they must walk.

They have nothing. And tonight, I, too, have nothing.

I am in their camp. I am their guest. I am here because I want to know their world, what they had and what they lost. For this one night, we share our lives.

The best way to get here is by Land Rover. My guide is a Western doctor. He gives introductions, then leaves for his own Christmas. It is now only I and them.

The name of this tribe is Touareg. They live in newcomers' tents on the banks of the Niger. They came in from the deep desert only a month ago, driven by hunger, refugees all.

I am taken to the the tent of the chief. He gives me his hand, he tells me his name. "Hamzata," he says.

I tell him mine. We smile at each other's foreignness, and it brings us closer.

Only one thing about him speaks of wealth - his turban. It is bright blue and of fine silk. It must be the only thing of value in this camp. He has as much pride in it as I in the three things that have gotten me through this trip - my L.L. Bean shirt, my Swiss army knife and Ray Ban sunglasses. Little items, perhaps, but treasured things that have been with me for years - things necessary in this desert, and right now, my only comfort.

The chief is well educated, fluent in French, but still, we share less than half a language. My French is only marginal. This night, there would be many gaps to bridge.

I watch them unfold the visitor's mat, and light a fire for tea, rituals now familiar to me. But unfamiliar, too. I am thinking only of home.

I miss some things. I miss the winter ocean. I miss music, and movies and the energy of the American spirit.

I wonder if it is snowing back home. Tree lights must be everywhere now. Here, I see only sand. Nearby, a tent of newcomers are settling to sleep without food. It is hard to feel the season in famine country.

I explain that it is Christmas Eve. I explain that in America, this is the best-loved of nights. They say they know about Christmas. It is not theirs, but they know it.

The chief motions to some of the others. He has them set up a special bed for me, in his tent. I tell him it's not necessary - it's bad enough I've imposed unannounced at 5 p.m. The ground would be fine. But he insists. I am his guest. It is important to him.

Soon, it begins to get cold. A fire is lit. I tell the chief I'm here to understand how his people came to be hungry.

It is simple, he says. They lived off cattle. The drought came. The grass disappeared. The cattle died.

"There must be more of a story than that," I say.

Yes, he says, there is. There is a story of loss here that speaks to all peoples who have lost something dear. But he did not want to take my time with it.

More tea is poured. More men come around. We gather close to the fire.

Why the desert, I ask. Americans would consider it a banishment.

That makes him smile. It is the opposite, he says. Desert, for them, is freedom itself. All men, he says, have an ache for land. With the nomad, it is only keener. It is why they choose not a piece of land, but a world of it. This way, they can even own night.

He began to tell me of the good times, the fat times. They were wealthy then. They'd have been wealthy even in America. Hamzata's family - just he and his brothers - owned 1,000 cows. Had he been born in Texas, he'd have been a rancher.

As his ancestors had for centuries, he too followed the rhythm of the desert. From October to May, they would find a stand of grass, and this would be the time of settlement. And it was a good time. But they could not shake the love of road, the need for road. Even the cattle knew the rhythm of this movement, and were themselves restless by June.

Now they would follow the time of wandering, a week here, a month there, the stars guiding them, the camps numbering 100 souls, though they did not call them camps, they were families.

And they brought with them a culture, hiring learned men to join them during the season of teaching. Always, from the sale of cows, there was money to buy comforts in town, where their wealth was regarded with awe. Good times. Fat times.

The chief did most of the talking. The others gave him the respect of their silence. I had to struggle with the French, but slowly, the same words were coming again and again.

"Avant." Before.

Before, when things were good, they had fresh steak every night, and fresh camel milk, too, which is the best of all milk. There was guitar music, and even hunts, the dogs tracking gazelles, the chiefs following on their horses.

"It sounds like the perfect life," I say.

Yes, says the chief. It was. Avant.

Before. Before the sun became a constant thing, the nurturer of life changing to the enemy of it, the grass curling under it, the animals beginning to die, dying year after year, until, last May, the last of them was gone. And a world gone with them.

"And now?" I ask.

Now they are trying to find a new way of living. They are trying to learn the cultivation of crop and a rootedness of their own. Now, there is no steak, only rice from UNICEF, and not always that. If the women sell their crafts in town, there is dinner. If not, there is none.

And around me, I can feel how it is ending. I can feel the ache of loss, the confusion of men and women who no longer have the things that make them what they are.

"Les peuples ont faim," says the chief. It is another phrase I would hear throughout the night. The people are hungry.

Soon, the cold becomes too much. We go into the tent. And he takes out an album of photographs. A nomad with a Polaroid.

He brings a lantern over and begins showing me what times looked like when times were good. His camels. . . his cows. . . his soul. It is important to him that I see this. He understands I am a journalist. This is for history, he says. So people will know there was once such a life.

I had expected we would sleep without food. But as we leaf through the album, I smell cooking.

He says it is because I am a stranger who cared enough to come. Tonight, there would be dinner, a true feast. They were preparing the meat from one of the last of their desert sheep, meat they'd until now been saving for more difficult times. The women bring it to the tent. The chief begins cutting the portions with a dull sword. I see he is having trouble, and offer him my Swiss army knife. He marvels at it and cuts the rest with ease.

Sixteen of us are in the tent. There is enough for each of us to have five bites. There is a seriousness to eating here, a respect for it that only people like this can know. The chief eats only half his portion. He insists I have the rest. He says he isn't hungry.

When it is done, we go back to seek the fire's warmth.

There is no talk for a while. Then I ask how hard this has been for them.

The chief says it is the hardest thing in experience, leaving the one life you know. Even the secrets understood only in their hearts are secrets that tie them to the desert. How do you give that away, he asks. How do you start over — not after a lifetime, but after an ancestry?

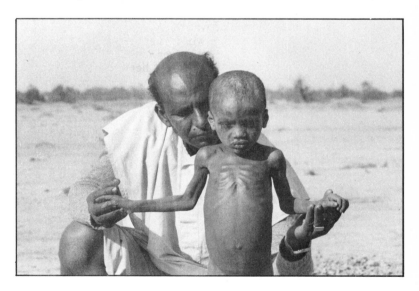

We stand and talk for more than an hour. I tighten my flannel shirt. I notice he is shivering.

"Is there no clothing?"

"If there is no food. . ." and he lets the sentence go at that.

More phrases become familiar with repetition. Rien a manger - nothing to eat. Or simply, rien.

Whenever I bend to take a note, two of the men bring lanterns to help me. Slowly, I begin to feel an unexpected kinship. We are all far from home.

There are only two beds in the tent, the

Hamzata, the chief, wanted to show me what hunger was doing to his people.

rest of the floor is sand. The chief takes one, I am given the other. At 10 p.m., we say good night. The lanterns are put out.

"La Noel joyeux," I say into the dark. "Tu comprends?"

"Ah, oui," he says. "Je comprends."

Christmas eve in the Sahara. I lie there for an hour, but cannot sleep. The cold comes into the tent, and into my bed. I walk outside for the embers of the fire. I am alone.

When this sky is clean, there is no sky like the Sahara sky. Under a full moon, you can read a newspaper. It helps me understand the draw of this place. When nature imposes a harshness, it seems to give back a beauty as great.

And now I find myself thinking about the things I've seen this month and what they mean.

What I've found here in this Touareg camp is what I've found everywhere: A man had a life he loved, the weather changed, and now he can't even feed his children.

I am where I'd begun in Ethiopia, in a tent city, hot by day and cold by night, where people of the land had gathered by force of weather, people now dependent on nations alone.

But here, as there, in the midst of this pain, I find a familiar twist of hope. There is a knowledge of spirit among famine victims here, a knowledge that says if you lose everything, you can still have civility, and there is wealth in that. I have never known the hospitality I've been given this night.

And I will always remember the hungry of Ethiopia, days from death, walking past a disabled food truck, ignoring its load of wheat, because touching it would have been theft.

I try again to sleep. I drift in and out. Finally, morning comes.

I recognize this morning. I have seen it before. It was the morning of the Korem feeding camp, at least on one level. Here, now, as happened there, the children come to me. I can walk nowhere without the children. And always, they grow quiet and content when I give them my hand.

Why is it that they, and the adults, too, are drawn to Americans so? I did not expect that. There is a warmth for our country I had not known existed. And it has nothing to do with politics or allegiances, only with what the people here see - that when there is pain, this nation reaches out.

And I realize more than ever before, that what we are, and what we stand for, rests with that compassion.

Before I leave, the chief wants me to see what I've come to see. We walk to the newcomers' tents. I notice he is squinting hard into the sun. Soon, we pause at one tent, and there, we find a true child of famine, one of the more troubled of this flock. The chief embraces him.

The child, to him, is a stranger. But to see the hurt in his face, it could be father and son. The little arms are so small. He holds him close long after I am finished with my photographs.

"Rien a manger," he says. "Rien a manger."

There is a kinship here Americans don't know. The greatest of this people feels truly diminished by the difficulties of the least of them.

I ask the chief about this. My French could not keep up with him, but I did not need it. I know, from a month in famine country, what he was saying. That we are one family here. Joined together by weather. And joined also by the little we have. The things we do not have are things that join us, for he who, like me, has nothing, is my family.

We hear the grind of an engine. A half mile distant, we see the doctor's Land Rover.

We walk back to the main camp. The chief tells me to wait, then disappears into his tent. Soon, he emerges. He is carrying his blue silk turban. He places it in my hands. For you, he says.

I take off my L.L. Bean shirt and hand it to him. Then I give him my Ray Ban sunglasses and Swiss army knife.

"For you," I say.

Christmas morning in the Sahara.

I climb into the Land Rover.

"Until next time," says the chief.

I say it, too. We begin to drive away.

As we do, I turn to look back at these people who have been changed but not broken by hunger.

And as I leave this place, I am thinking one thought.

One world. ▪▪▪

"There is a knowledge of spirit among famine victims here, a knowledge that says if you lose everything, you can still have civility, and there is wealth in that".

Even more than the scenes of pain, I will hold onto this scene of hope: the chief, pouring water into the desert, trying to begin anew.

All author's royalties from the sale of "An African Journey" will be donated to two organizations Mark Patinkin observed at work in Africa - Doctors Without Borders, and Foster Parents Plan International. The groups were chosen because they address the twin answers to Africa's food problems: emergency relief and long-term development.

Doctors Without Borders, based in France, is perhaps the key medical force in the continent's most difficult areas. The physicians are paid $400 a month.

Foster Parents Plan International spends $60 million a year on operations around the world, including eight African countries. The group blends a humanitarian approach of sponsoring children with an emphasis on village-by-village development. Their projects range from tree farms and irrigation efforts to schools and health centers.

Doctors Without Borders
68 Boulevard St.
Marcel Paris 5E 75005

Foster Parents Plan
International
155 Plan Way
Warwick, RI 02887

Church World Service
475 Riverside Drive
New York, N.Y. 10115

Lutheran World Relief
360 Park Ave. S.
New York, N.Y. 10010

American Jewish Joint
Distribution Committee
Suite 1914, Dept. M,
60 East 42nd St.
New York, New York,
10165

Save The Children
Ethiopia Fund
P.O. Box 925
Westport, Conn. 06881

Oxfam America
115 Broadway
Boston, Mass. 02110

U.S. Committee for UNICEF
Box 3040
Grand Central Station
New York, N.Y. 10163

Partnership for Productivity
International.
2001 S. St. NW. Suite 610.
Washington, DC. 20009.

CARE
Campaign for Africa
P.O. Box 645
Boston, Mass. 02116

Catholic Relief Services
P.O. Box 2045
Church Street Station
New York, N.Y. 10008

World Vision
African Drought
P.O. Box 'O'
Pasadena, CA 91109

▼

Mark Patinkin, 32, is a Chicago native and 1974 graduate of Middlebury College in Vermont. He spent the next two years as a reporter with the Utica Daily Press in upstate New York. He came to the Providence Journal-Bulletin as a general assignment reporter in 1976. He has been writing a column four times a week for the past six years. His columns are carried on the Scripps-Howard news wire. He lives in Providence, R.I.